JODIE

JODIE

A Biography

Louis Chunovic

CB

CONTEMPORARY BOOKS

A TRIBUNE COMPANY

Library of Congress Cataloging-in-Publication Data

Chunovic. Louis.
   Jodie: a biography / Louis Chunovic.
      p.   cm.
   Filmography: p.
   ISBN 0-8092-3404-1 (cloth)
   ISBN 0-8092-3138-7 (paper)
      1. Foster, Jodie.   2. Actors—United States—Biography.
I. Title.
PN2287.F624C58   1995
791.43'028'092—dc20
   [B]   95-21509
                                                              CIP

Cover and interior design by Kim Bartko

Published by Contemporary Books, Inc.
Two Prudential Plaza, Chicago, Illinois 60601-6790
Manufactured in the United States of America
International Standard Book Number: 0-8092-3404-1 (cloth)
                                    0-8092-3138-7 (paper)
10   9   8   7   6   5   4   3   2   1

for Alicia

"I'm used to being analyzed, dissected, turned around, put in places. That kind of thing says a lot more about the reviewer than it does about the subject. It's fine with me."

JODIE FOSTER
INTERVIEW, OCTOBER 1991

"If God had designed a perfect acting machine, it would be pretty close to Jodie."

JON AMIEL, DIRECTOR
VANITY FAIR, MAY 1994

Contents

ACKNOWLEDGMENTS

MY THANKS TO LINDA Gray of Contemporary Books, who originally suggested this project to me, trusted me to write it without interference, then graciously and efficiently guided the manuscript past legal brambles and permissions thickets to publication.

INTRODUCTION

| *Interview and Overview*

IT WAS THE USUAL
hack-and-flack deal, the kind reporters cut with press agents every
day in the company town of Hollywood: If he'd come with a camera crew to cover the party for the posh private school being held
at her client's, a struggling local nightclub, the PR woman
promised the TV news reporter she'd "give it" to him "exclusive."

Celebrity parents would be there, she assured him, and the
year's Best Actress Oscar winner—a graduate of the private high
school—had RSVPed, too. In fact, she was the evening's cochair.

RSVPS were sucker bait, the TV reporter knew. Half the time
they didn't show up. It was just a way to get the press out.

Still, May 2, 1989, was a slow night on the entertainment beat,
and it was always better to be out, self-assigned and trolling for
sound bites, than to just hang around the newsroom and wait for
something to go wrong.

The TV reporter had covered the big Oscar show just a month

earlier. He'd been one of the hundreds of reporters and photographers lining the long red carpet leading into the Shrine Auditorium from the street where the limos stopped. It was tightly stage-managed pandemonium. Even TV crews from outfits with enough clout to get good camera positions were reduced to shouting inane questions at passing movie stars, hoping the Hollywood royalty would make a momentary stop to favor them with a response, a smile. On the makeshift bleachers behind, delirious fans, some of whom had camped there overnight, screamed out their names.

He well remembered the young Best Actress's acceptance speech, easily the most eloquent of the bloated, self-congratulatory night—"*This is such a big deal,*" she had begun, "*and my life is so simple.*" The possibility of a one-on-one interview was worth the time and the twenty-minute drive over to Century City, to the new club on the site of the defunct Playboy Club, where the party was being held.

On any given Tinseltown evening, there's a plethora of parties and premieres for the entertainment press to choose from. On a showbiz scale of newsworthiness or cachet, the twenty-fifth anniversary celebration of Le Lycée Français de Los Angeles, a bilingual private school known for its rigorous discipline and classical education, was distinctly a minor event. Without the Best Actress "exclusive," the reporter knew, the lycée's *anniversaire* was not worth the videotape it would take to cover—not even with the "bites" from the promised celebrity parents.

Inside the low-ceilinged nightclub decorated with weaving towers of orange and black balloons an incongruously loud steel drum band was pumping reggae music out over a soigné crowd that looked more attuned to light opera. The guests, men in conservative suits, women in expensive little black cocktail dresses, sipped from champagne flutes as they swirled about the narrow entrance hall, making polite chitchat while gazing in cultivated wonderment at the blowups of school yearbook photos covering the painted-black wall and trying to ignore the TV camera's intrusive bright light.

There that night were a gracious and glowing Ruth Pointer, of the Pointer Sisters singing group, who said she'd enrolled her daughter at Le Lycée for "the discipline," and actress Theresa Russell, who specialized in tragic bombshell roles (even playing Marilyn Monroe once), particularly in pictures directed by her husband, Nicolas Roeg (*Insignificance*, *Track 29*, among others).

Getting B-roll, it was called—shots to cut to between individual sound bites—and the reporter wanted plenty of it: various images of the partying crowd, the bartenders pouring drinks, the band jumpin', pull-ins and push-outs on the black-and-white photos, particularly the one of the Best Actress as valedictorian of her minuscule high school class. The newly graduated students had been photographed in caps and gowns with her in the middle of the group, her mortarboard at a jaunty angle over her confident Cali Girl face and shiny blond hair. Not a trace was visible of the troubled loners and tough street kids she'd already made a career of playing. Her expression was one of gazing into the future, and now, thought the reporter, the future was here.

Outside, on the sidewalk of the ABC Entertainment Center, the de rigueur red carpet and red velvet rope were guarded by a scowling, erstwhile Fabio figure with big hair, big muscles, and a bodybuilder's cramped-looking, arm-swinging walk. He was wearing a Michael Jackson–style black-and-silver jumpsuit; next to him, a thin, nervous ponytailed man, almost lost in an oversized suit, was checking off names on a clipboard.

Arriving, she would have been easy to miss, just another immaculately put-together woman, no more than five-four, her shoulder-length honey-blond hair tightly pulled back and held by a black velvet bow. Designer tortoiseshell spectacles and tastefully simple pearl-drop earrings framed her face, with its strong jaw and slightly aquiline nose, more famous now than at any time since she was eighteen. She, too, was wearing a variation of the evening's uniform: tailored black skirt and matching jacket over a white silk blouse.

In the increasingly crass and cutthroat world of southern California television, the tabloidization of television news, not yet much remarked on, was nonetheless well under way. And that meant two things: one, the old standards of decorum among the press were out the window; two, the picture was everything. These days the first rule was *get 'em on tape before they disappear.*

The cameraman, a seen-it-all, shot-it-all pro, had been told to roll as soon as she appeared. On a nod and a pointed finger, he flooded the nightclub entrance with harsh TV-news light, pinning the Best Actress even before she got inside.

Just a flash of exasperation crossed her face, away from the spotlight as classically American as the conservative suit she'd put on for this occasion. She had every right to be expecting a private night, but this was a trouper of legendary proportions, and she instantly slipped her eyeglasses into her leather shoulder bag, turning with a dazzling smile to meet the press.

"WHO'S IT FOR?" she asks directly, eyeing the camera. The reporter names a local Los Angeles TV station. "Will you talk to us for a second?"

The Best Actress shrugs. "OK."

The reporter knows just where he wants to set up. For as long as it takes them to get inside and stationed in front of the graduation photo showing the Best Actress as teenage valedictorian, the cameraman turns off his light. But as soon as she is looking at the photo of herself and her high school classmates, all in their caps and gowns, all gazing optimistically out at the unknown, the reporter makes a circular "let's rev-it-up and roll" motion with his finger, and back on the glaring camera light comes.

Smiling, the Best Actress turns to face the camera.

"What's that do for you?" the reporter asks peremptorily, pointing at her class picture on the wall.

When it came to the press, the Best Actress had long had a seemingly contradictory reputation: guarded about certain subjects, completely open, even voluble, about the rest. She can talk and talk, and you'd swear you were getting the straight dope, reporters would marvel privately, but when you listen to the tape or read over your notes, you find she said nothing that wasn't straight out of the press kit, nothing she hadn't said a hundred times before.

"I don't know," she begins thoughtfully. It's as though if only you could get a little closer to her reflective pale blue eyes you would see her mind whirring transparently. "It brings back a lot of memories. It's the first time I've ever seen this picture actually, to tell you the truth. What I remember—"

As she speaks, the camera cuts to the black-and-white graduation photo itself, beginning with a full shot of the grouped students, then slowing pushing in until only she is visible in extreme close-up. Then a quick cut back to the Best Actress again on camera:

"—is having stitches in my chin two days before I graduated. I fell on a tennis court, so I had all these black things sticking out of my chin."

Pointing to her chin, she scrunches up her face girlishly. "I was very, very embarrassed about that."

"Is that the first thing that came to your mind when you looked at the picture?" The reporter sounds a little disappointed, as if to say "Is that *all?*" It's a typical reporter trick and a typical reporter question.

"It was, actually," the Best Actress replies. "Those black stitches." In great good humor, she shakes her head at the memory. "It was great. It certainly paved the way for a lot of my thoughts. It taught me a lot of things."

"What was the advantage to you of going to this school?" asks the reporter.

"Oh, let's see. A lot of people would say the facility with languages," replies the Best Actress, who's famously bilingual. "You know, the French system, which is very rigorous and strict and all of that. But more importantly, it suited my personality, because it taught me to read—by that I mean *largely*," she adds with a big, glowing smile. "You know, analyzing things and dissecting things."

She is also famously workaholic and focused. "Is that where you learned discipline?" the reporter wants to know.

She seems surprised by the question, looking askance at her interlocutor. "No," she replies, "to tell the truth I discipline myself so much I couldn't imagine anybody could discipline me more." She laughs, a throaty, musical sound. "I *responded* to it; a lot of people don't. I responded to it very well."

She rocks back on her heels, smiles directly into the camera, glances to the side. Extricating yourself from a conversation you don't want to be having is hard enough in so-called real life; under the unblinking gaze of a television news camera, it's next to impossible.

If this had been a premiere or a photo-op arrival at some show-biz charity event, someone—a hovering press agent—would have been at the Best Actress's elbow at her slightest sign to smile and scrape and say to the reporter, "Just one more question" or "I'm sorry, Miss Foster, but we've got to move along. Thank you so very much." And she would be gone.

But tonight, there's no one to stop the reporter from plunging ahead. "Let's talk about that little gold statuette you recently won," he continues recklessly. "Will you repeat for our viewers what you said you were going to do with it the next day?"

Jodie Foster looks intrigued; on her face, a puzzled frown.

"You remember?" the reporter asks.

"No." She rocks back, fixing him with her famous, big-eyed tough girl look. "What'd I say I was gonna with it?" she challenges. "*You* tell *me*."

"OK. You were going to take it to the video store and . . ."

In the few weeks since Oscar night it's become a well-known

story, another example of the "normal" life she so obviously wants to believe she can lead: the Best Actress, a videoaholic, declaring on Oscar night that a clerk at her local video store promised her a free rental if she won and brought in the statuette.

Aha! "Yes, I was, as a matter of fact." Her face lights up. "Well, I *didn't* take it to the video store, because that evening it was taken away from my hands by my family." She seems in high spirits now. "Actually, I didn't see it again for another week." She laughs, then delivers the punch line directly into the camera. "But yeah, I got free videos, and that made my night."

Again, it's an exit line, but again the reporter asks another question. "How'd it change your life?"

The Best Actress seems surprised, perhaps because the reporter isn't following standard operating procedure. She's told her Oscar anecdote, reminisced about Le Lycée. In modern Hollywood, there's a hello-I-must-be-going protocol for encounters like this— a few jolly seconds, then it's on down the red carpet, waving at the unseen masses until safely inside the confines of the premiere or other mandatory glittering event; anything else in the way of interviews is negotiated first, with concessions expected, of course.

Just a hint of a wary look crosses her face: What else does this guy want?

"What?" she asks.

"The Oscar," says the reporter. "You know, you're Best Actress this year . . ."

"It makes me a lot more comfortable with how much I like to be alone," she replies. "I actually spent the first two weeks after getting the Oscar with my family, you know, in jogging clothes, kind of drinking champagne, eating caviar." She giggles, giving an endearing cross-eyed, goofy shrug. "And my nephew said, 'Good fish, Mommy.' You know, it made my—" she shrugs, nods, obviously looking for just the proper phrase, the appropriate passage of time—"six months."

She laughs, but there's something else on the reporter's mind, and he greets her witty remark with a frown, prompting her to go on. "I'm sure that someday I'll be out of work again," she adds, all seriousness now. "I've been in this business a long time." An understatement: she's been earning a living in show business since infancy. "So it means exactly what it's supposed to mean, which is a lot of jobs for the next five years."

It's a good answer, classic even, and the reporter should be grateful for it. But he hasn't even been listening really. In a time of shifting news values and priorities, he's wondering instead about the public's right to know. For so much of her early career, particularly as a distinctly and refreshingly non–sugar 'n' spice 'n' everything nice little girl on TV and in the movies, she'd been emblematic of the zeitgeist, but she'd also been dogged by it, and dangerously too. Now another irony: her greatest triumph—the brave Oscar-winning performance that revived, perhaps saved, her career—has coincided with another ratcheting down of prevailing standards as part of the tabloidization of American pop culture. Communism may be collapsing all across Eastern Europe, but on the evening news Zsa Zsa's cop-slapping trial is the lead story. The evolving new rule: *anything goes, and gossip is king.*

Therefore, should he ask about her father, who'd abandoned the family shortly before Foster was born and from whom she'd been almost totally estranged her entire life? There's recently been an aborted attempt at reconciliation, but gossip has it that the motive behind the planned reunion was actually money. (A few days later, as it turned out, her father was the focus of a local newspaper story that portrayed Foster as "beset by family problems," just when she "should be happiest," because a "Superior Court judge ordered [her] father to return $75,000 to two Beverly Hills residents who invested with him. . . . Now the two women who sued him have hired a detective to try to determine if he has assets to pay them the money he owes."[1])

Does he dare ask about the rumors—the scurrilous rumors— he and his colleagues in various newsrooms have been gossiping carelessly about for months? How can he? After all, when he'd recently had the chance, he'd been unable to bring himself to ask Richard Gere, "About those gerbils, Rich . . ."

That particular rumor had even already broken into print, with a coy reference in a local newspaper's gossip column. It was false but so widely believed in Hollywood that members of the fourth estate finally had called around to hospital emergency rooms: "Tell me, Doc, you hear of any gay men showing up with small rodents inserted up their, ahem, backsides?"

Another TV reporter, one who worked for one of the tabloid shows, was now saying that Foster had stormed out of an interview after being asked about the "Big Fight on the Set" story. It was the latest elaboration of The Rumor, a much-discussed bit of gossip purporting that the two costars of *The Accused* had been lovers but fought over another woman, a pop diva whose subsequent marriage wasn't even enough to stop the "informed" speculation. After all, the argument went, *Rock Hudson* had been married. Dish-crazy Hollywood was as certain of the reality of the Big Fight as it had been about the gerbils. So what the reporter finds himself uncomfortably wrestling with is the urge to ask if it's true.

Instead, pressing on while the Best Actress runs a hand lightly across her smooth cap of pulled-back blond hair, now looking back at him curiously, he prompts: "About being alone: I'm surprised you can tolerate being alone. Most people can't."

"Oh, I don't know about that," she responds, seemingly taken aback by the very suggestion. "I enjoy it, always have. I was one of those boring little kids. I'm a boring person actually," she adds, perhaps at some level intuiting where this could be going. She looks directly into the camera again. "*Believe me,*" she says, her eyes twinkling with amusement.

IT'S A CONCEIT so charmingly put that even the cameraman laughed. At that moment we were both entranced, just as so many others in our profession have been both before and since.

Since it was Le Lycée's anniversary party, I asked if she'd like to say something in French for our home viewing audience, and she demurred, quite sensibly, because that would make her feel like a kid going to Grandma's house and being asked to perform for the adults. Fair enough.

It was over. To keep her pinned by the TV light any longer would be pointless and rude. I asked a final quick question about her plans (she said she didn't have any, hadn't found a role she liked yet), thanked her for giving us so much time, and we shook hands. I turned and ran a finger across my throat. Cut.

The merciless light went out, freeing Jodie Foster to join her party at last, while the shooter and I packed up and headed back to seedy Hollywood.

AFTER NEARLY TWO decades in sunny, smoggy, sprawling Los Angeles, mostly on the Hollywood beat, I believe I have nary an illusion left when it comes to the denizens of Tinseltown.

Call it too much time behind the curtain, observing as the agents and the producers, the lawyers and the press agents, and all the other power-lunching wizards of the present day happily pull at the levers of the dream machine. The beautiful people indeed!

I've seen too much attitude and cynicism, too much bad behavior, too much single-minded careerism that would do a shark in the water proud. The makers of popular culture are its first and most complete victims, a poet once said. Too true! They believe the hype.

No surprise, then, that here in the home of larger-than-life cinematic heroes and heroines, I'm running out of heroes of my own. That's why I was so pleased to be approached to write a biography of actor/director/producer Jodie Foster. It wasn't just the two Best Actress Oscars she'd won that captured my admiration, either.

I had a sense that this was a remarkable woman, that for once maybe I should believe the hype.

At the publisher they didn't know that I had met her. Twice.

One you already know about. The second time was some months later, at a club in Hollywood, I believe, on the Sunset Strip. I'd just spent all day covering the latest coming of some rock god—I think it was David Bowie, master of the timely transformation, but there were so many gigs to cover in those days that I can't be sure. I remember Bowie was in town then with a new look, a new sound, and a "garage band" called Tin Machine. Improbably, two of comedian Soupy Sales's sons were part of the small ensemble that played gritty, basic, bop-till-you-drop rock and roll.

They were playing one of those "unannounced" gigs at a small club on the Strip, the kind that gets touted by the radio and attracts rabid fans by the thousands, all lining up around the block hoping to score one of the few hundred available tickets. It had been typical bedlam; there had been the first show to tape, then a live shot for the news. I'd been all over the packed little club with a camera and a microphone. Now it was over, and I was kicking back with some buddies from the station, waiting for the start of the late show to watch Bowie and company do their thing.

Although I'm in some doubt about which tiny, smoky club it was exactly (conventional wisdom about the sixties applies just as well to the Hollywood club scene: if you can remember all the details, you weren't really there), I do remember looking around, checking it all out. Off in the back, half hidden from view, a little blond rock-and-roller and a dark-haired, dark-complected, smoldery-looking guy were entwined. After a moment, I caught Jodie Foster's eye.

She nodded. I went over and said hello. We shook hands, exchanged pleasantries, I reminded her where we'd met, and she introduced me to the dark-haired young man. I don't remember his name, but I do remember thinking at the time, So much for rumors and simple-minded labels.

There's something special about Foster that's at once transparent and mysterious. You can see it in her eyes. You can see it on the big screen; you could see it even in her demeanor when, as a child, she performed on TV. I'd seen it that one time I'd interviewed her, some years ago, right after she won her first Academy Award. It was an intelligence, a *wary* intelligence.

"She's damn good. She's a young Bette Davis." That's how Bette Davis herself once described Jodie Foster.[2] That tart-tongued speaker ought to know.

After all, here is someone who practically was born into the business, albeit at its periphery, but has seemingly managed to remain independent of it—all the while doing exemplary work; someone around whom controversy and gossip have swirled but who's somehow, almost miraculously, never been tainted by it.

In many ways Jodie Foster has led an exemplary life and is an exemplary person. That's why the two common reactions by the people who knew I was writing this book have given me pause.

"You gonna stalk her?" was one frequent joking response, but the question that every single person asked was this:

"You gonna out her?"

I thought about it. To the first question the uncomfortable answer is a reluctant "In a way, yes, I suppose I am."

This is not the authorized story, sanctioned and sanitized, but, partly because of my sense of who Jodie Foster is, this is biography at a distance. Rather than listen to the canned encomiums of self-interested careerists or the poisonous whispers of shadowy anonymous sources, I've stalked Jodie Foster through computers, card catalogs, and microfiche, basing this story on the voluminous public record of nearly three decades in the public eye.

I did write a letter to her shortly after her thirty-second birthday, telling her about this book, asserting my intention to do "honorable" work, and asking for an interview during the period when she'd be out publicizing *Nell* anyway. Not surprisingly, there was no reply. Once word got around that I was doing this book, people on both coasts contacted me with claims about affairs and other personal intimacies. Sometimes I listened, mostly I didn't; nothing was verifiable in the traditional journalistic sense.

Despite having previously practiced it, I've always had my doubts about the biographer's art. For one thing, it's too reductive.

Particularly when it comes to writing about a living, feeling person, I share many of Janet Malcolm's scruples, while aspiring to I. F. Stone's methods. (I share Malcolm's scruples about journalism, too, but as I've seen it practiced, the problem is not treachery so much as it is co-optation.) There's no reason that what worked so beautifully for Stone in Washington—interpreting the nuggets found in a diligent search of the public record—can't work in Hollywood, too. If there's a "fair" way to tell a celebrity's story—from a vantage point higher than that of the gutter and also somewhat more distanced than the view afforded from inside the celebrity's pocket—then, I'm convinced, that is it.

So here you will find the films and the life and an interpretation of both. Much of it in Jodie Foster's own words.

To the second question, the one that sprang first and foremost to absolutely everyone's lips, I plead indifference.

To the activists who threatened to "out" her over *The Silence of the Lambs*, to my acquaintances who professed outrage—How could *she* OF ALL PEOPLE act in a movie with that homophobe?—when she agreed to do the big-screen western spoof *Maverick*, and especially to my fellow journalists and the headline writers who have dogged her career with innuendo while almost never daring to speak the dread *l* word, I say that common decency and respect for the varieties of sexuality, both homo- and hetero-, require us not to label her.

But never fear, gentle reader. I know my penultimate responsibility is to you.

KID STUFF

The Coppertone Kid

AT THE AGE WHEN
most little girls are lavishing full attention on their first Barbie,
three-year-old Alicia Christian Foster, known from infancy on as
Jodie, was a universally recognized all-American icon.

In the mid-sixties she was the original Coppertone kid on TV,
that sunny symbol of summertime innocence, a glowing blond
toddler cutely caught with pale bottom bared as a puppy tugged
her swimsuit down.

The Kid was born on November 19, a year before gunfire in
Dallas ended Camelot. The sixties—the tune-in, turn-on, dropout sixties, the takin'-it-to-the-street sixties, the sixties of the Fab
Four, Vietnam, and women's liberation—were just getting under
way.

Jodie, the youngest of four children, was born into what had
become a single-parent household a few months before. Her
father, Lucius Foster III, an air force officer and a Yale graduate,

had left her mother, Evelyn Almond Foster—known universally as Brandy—after ten years of marriage.

According to an account published more than a quarter of a century later, Brandy, who'd moved to Los Angeles in the fifties from Rockford, Illinois, discovered that she was pregnant again on the same day she appeared in divorce court.[1]

Looking for a way to keep the family financially secure after the separation, Brandy, a sometime film press agent who was savvy about show business, began taking her oldest child and only son, Lucius IV, nicknamed Buddy, out for auditions. Soon he was working steadily, eventually becoming a regular on the TV series "Mayberry R.F.D.," from which he brought in some $25,000 a year.[2]

Baby Jodie "spoke full sentences when she was twelve months old, and you could reason with her," said her mother. "She taught herself to read at three. . . . At five she could go in cold and audition like an adult."[3]

In her late teens Foster recalled her childhood growing up in the sixties as a time when her mother "always had us making placards and marching in peace demonstrations.

"I could wear the same clothes all week, and she wouldn't mind as long as I was happy. . . .

"I feel lucky in a way that I never knew a father, that there was never a marital conflict in the house. I've always felt like . . . I took the place of a husband, roommate, or a pal."[4]

In the course of almost three decades Jodie Foster has been interviewed hundreds of times and been questioned on subjects from the frivolous to the profound. Her resentment at her birth father's abandonment of his family was obviously painful but hardly a secret; for many years it was a regular feature of stories about her, as was the conflict between being "normal" and being "special," and her insistence that being an actor was just one job among many on a film crew and that making pictures was just another up-before-dawn blue-collar job.

Her "luck" at being born into a single-parent household in the sixties was a theme she kept returning to as well. Years later her mother sounded the theme succinctly: "It was just at the beginning of women's liberation, and she kind of personified that in a child. She had a strength and an uncoquettishness. Maybe it comes from being raised without a father to say, 'Turn around and show Daddy how pretty you look.'"[5]

Jodie's career began as one of those bedazzling Hollywood flukes: Her older brother, Buddy, then the only child actor in the Foster clan, was auditioning for the part of the Coppertone kid himself. Mom didn't have a sitter for Jodie, and she didn't want to leave the child alone outside in the car.

"I wouldn't go anywhere without my brother. . . . When they told him to take off his shirt, I was behind him," Foster recalled as a woman in her late twenties, "and I took my shirt off, too, and did my muscles like he did—because I loved my brother. They said, 'What's your name, little girl?'"[6]

Despite the fact that her brother was five years older than she, the agency people took one look at little Jodie and changed the campaign on the spot, from one that centered around a little boy to one based on an even littler girl. The rest was, at least in the beginning, history of the predictably wonderful dream factory sort.

Cookies, breakfast cereal, dog food, toothpaste, potato chips, and some four dozen other products followed, from Ken-L Ration to Oreos—"I remember . . . having to eat sickening things all day, and throwing up. After being in a shampoo ad," she said, "I couldn't get the shit out of my hair for ten days."[7] But the suntan-lotion advertising campaign had greased the way to a lucrative career in commercials for Foster while she was still a preschooler, leading one writer at the time to label her the "mini-queen of commercials"[8] when she was just into grade school. Eating junk food on cue to the point of nausea and vomiting may be justly horrifying to most parents, but the money paid the bills and, arguably, kept the Foster family together. Jodie's recollections of those years are almost totally loving, and her mother remained not only her manager and confidante but also her best friend for years.

When she was eight, her mother enrolled Jodie in a private Los Angeles school, Le Lycée Français, known then as now as the establishment of choice where children of celebrities could get a rigorous classical education.

"At the start of the third grade, when she still attended public school, Jodie was tested for the state's gifted program," recalled her mother almost two decades later. "When the school saw the results, they wanted to skip her [into a higher grade] . . . and they wanted to push her into science. I didn't want her skipped. I wanted her challenge to be another language. So I took her out of public school and enrolled her at the Lycée."[9]

She was formally a student there through high school, although she was often physically away on a set or on a location. By law all child actors have to receive an education while they're working, and that means on-set teachers and schoolwork. "I would do twenty minutes of math, then be called to the set to do a scene, then do forty minutes of English, then be called back to the set," she said later of those early days. "I learned how to have an immediate sense of concentration."[10]

Le Lycée's director, who doubled as an on-location tutor for Jodie on the set of at least one movie, called her "intelligent, hard-working and the most well-balanced child I have ever known. . . . To the rest of the world, Jodie is an object of curiosity and speculation, but at school, fortunately, she is among many children of film stars. They help her to be normal."[11] The "normal" young Mademoiselle Foster went on to become both high school class valedictorian and editor of the school newspaper.

Years later, when he first met the then-teenage Foster in November 1976, at a café in New York's Pierre hotel, no less a celebrity-smitten authority on pop culture than artist Andy Warhol pronounced himself "really impressed" to learn that she was the original Coppertone kid.[12]

The Coppertone ad was her first professional job, and through it she had an impact on the country's consciousness that she wouldn't match for a decade, not until the all-American kid's transformation into Iris, the teenybopper hooker tottering down the mean streets on six-inch platform shoes in Martin Scorsese's landmark film *Taxi Driver*.

In fact, according to *Taxi Driver*'s screenwriter, Paul Schrader, he and director Scorsese were aware of a study examining "subliminal incitements to rape. Researchers had been surprised that, in group therapy, rapists often mentioned Foster's Coppertone ad. . . . As Schrader summarized the analysis by psychologists, the ad indeed had a prurient dimension: 'It had just the right mixture for these rapists of adolescent sexuality, female nudity, rear entry, animals, and violence.' "[13]

That her first public exposure, as a mere infant, should have called forth this litany of violation was a dark irony indeed.

Although there are many things that Jodie Foster has resolutely refused to discuss in public, while spending virtually her entire life in the public view, it's an irony that can't have been lost on the student of modern literature and dramatic narrative that she soon became.

Television Roles

IN TELEVISIONLAND

imitation is not just the sincerest form of flattery; it's the preferred business practice, too.

This was as true more than two decades ago as it is today, and in November 1973 ABC announced plans to turn Peter Bogdanovich's knockabout film comedy *Paper Moon*, starring the father/daughter team of Ryan and Tatum O'Neal as a con man and a wised-up nine-year-old in the Depression thirties, into a TV series.

It was no surprise that the wiser-than-her-tender-years kid part went to feisty little Jodie Foster. Who better?

The little kid was a pro, a quick study in the unforgiving school of hard knocks that is American commercial television. She was also developing what, much later, she called her "technician qualities. . . . I love those years, and I'm really happy I did them."[14]

Despite the brutal pace, despite the financial strictures and the technical limitations of the medium, she was thriving. Her track record already included a lucrative career doing commercials and more than a dozen TV guest shots.

Shows she appeared on included the TV version of *Bob & Carol & Ted & Alice*, "Bonanza," "The Courtship of Eddie's Father," "Gunsmoke," "Julia," "Medical Center," "My Three Sons," "Nanny and the Professor," "The Partridge Family," and the short-lived "The Paul Lynde Show." In the last, a single-season series about a lawyer and his "infuriating" family, she turned up in one episode as a kid in a commune.[15] (Because it was the early seventies, and the high schools and colleges were overflowing with boomers, liberation and counterculture were in the air, becoming regular fodder for and foils on sitcoms of the period, so the lure of communes could be played for comedy, and the audience would understand. Good sitcom kids were always being tempted by, and rejecting, the blandishments of the tie-dyed never-trust-anyone-over-thirty crowd in these shows. Ironically, and appropriately, in Jodie Foster's great breakthrough picture of the midseventies, *Taxi Driver*, it's her character's ambition to escape the mean streets for a commune in Vermont.)

In 1972 there had even been a failed half-hour pilot for CBS, "My Sister Hank," in which she played the title role. In the one episode that aired, Henrietta "Hank" Bennett was a pretty tomboy trying to overcome the discrimination that kept her out of Little League because of her gender.[16]

Her media-wise mom had already decreed no more commercials and no more bit parts for her daughter, and she had upped Jodie's price from the standard $450 per week to a then-unheard-of $1,000.[17]

Jodie had a reputation as a pro, and the little TV vet was riding a hot streak on the big screen, too, with four pictures in two years.

She also brought to the table the same mature Hollywood-kid quality that would win Tatum O'Neal a Best Supporting Actress Oscar for the original film version of *Paper Moon*. It was a quality that adjective-addicted reviewers could readily dismiss as mere feistiness, but it went deeper.

All through her childhood reviewers noticed something—"a gravity beyond her years," "a connectedness to the real world," "self-assured and determined."

As *Foxes* director Adrian Lyne put it years later, "It was strange. . . . You felt that she was more mature than her mother."[18]

That assessment was shared by James Komack, whose company coproduced "The Courtship of Eddie's Father," in which he also costarred as Norman, the show's aging-hipster second banana. Jodie's mom was "just a good-lookin', easygoin' woman who was no match for her kid," he said.[19]

When it came to little girls acting, Foster and O'Neal represented something new—not so much tomboys as children of the changing times. The effects of both the women's movement and the counterculture were reverberating in early-seventies TV land.

Looking back on it all from a teenager's vantage point a few years later, Jodie Foster said, "I hate the idea that everybody thinks if a kid's going to be an actress it means she has to play Shirley Temple or someone's little sister. That's not reality anymore."[20]

And even later, as a twentysomething young woman reflecting back,[21] it seemed to her that "I never felt that I was stereotyped into a child role, so I really didn't have to make any transformation from child to woman."[21]

In her TV guest shots, Jodie was as likely to take a punch at a little boy, which she did, for example, in her single "Partridge Family" outing, as she was to kiss the smitten lad. That was true, too, in her recurring role as Joey Kelly, a tough little seven-year-old girl without a mother, in "The Courtship of Eddie's Father." For example, in one episode Joey's schoolyard greeting to little Eddie is to trip him as he walks past.

Joey's father, Joe, is a typically helpless, clueless, but essentially decent and gruffly affectionate sitcom man, and his little daughter proudly cooks and cares for him. In one 1970 episode she shows up to stay at Eddie's house for the weekend (her father is away in the army reserves, we learn; with the Vietnam War on the network evening news every night, it was a typical TV series touch in that period), carrying her own suitcase and wearing a red-and-blue sailor's dress. The gap-toothed blond moppet, like some latter-day Goldilocks, announces solemnly that "nobody has to take care of me. I can take care of myself."

Later, when Eddie (Brandon Cruz) asks Joey if she wants to play, she fixes her startling pale-blue eyes on his prized fish tank. "Can I play with your fish?" she asks innocently. And when the little boy condescends to the little girl, Joey retorts, as she gives him a convincingly solid smack on the upper arm: "Whaddya think I am, Eddie Corbett"—SMACK!—"stupid?"

After eyeing the fish tank once more with some degree of thwarted mischievous longing, she says at the end of the episode, when her pixilated dad has come to retrieve her, "Hey, Pop, let's go home now. I'll fix you a beer."

Another time, when Eddie is away at weekend camp, his father's plans for a romantic weekend are thwarted when little Joey again shows up with her suitcase, announcing that her dad and his girl-friend have gone to Las Vegas to get married. Says little Joey, offer-

ing to make dinner for Eddie's father, in a line that must have resonated with little Jodie: because no ladies are hanging about, they
can be "just a kid and a dad." And later, after dinner, when
they're doing dishes, she says with a convincing wistful gravity,
"With Pop and me it was always magic."

As in this moment with Eddie's father (Bill Bixby), in any
scene with an adult, of the two she was likely to seem the more
mature one and to deliver the most adult line readings.

Take, for example, the episode of "Kung Fu" entitled "Alethea."
Shot at the Fox Ranch in Malibu over the course of a single hec-
tic week in February 1973 by noted film director John Badham,
who went on to direct such pictures as *Saturday Night Fever*, *War
Games*, and *Stakeout* but was then just starting out in TV,
"Alethea" is a *Rashomon*-like meditation on the loss of innocence.

Foster played the title character—twelve-year-old Alethea Patri-
cia Ingram, a spunky child of the Old West, with big pale-blue
eyes, apple cheeks, and a winning, crooked smile.

This was no typical child actor's turn, relying on ingratiating
cuteness to make us ignore our curmudgeonly disbelief. There's
something tough and grown-up about this little blond girl. In her
eyes you can see her character think.

As soon as the ten-year-old girl came into the audition, director Badham could see it too: "This beautiful child who was very
skinny, [with] long, skinny, twiglike legs, who had a short white
summer dress on, there was something extremely modern about
the way that she moved. She was very alert; you just were immediately very struck by her."

Badham remembers going home during the shoot and saying
to his wife: "'You're not going to believe this, but I've got a crush
on a ten-year-old girl.' I said, 'Believe it or not, there's something
very sexy about her.'"

It wasn't that she was a flirt or coquettish the way that some
needy child actors can be, says Badham. "Never. There was not a
flirty bone in her body. . . . It was just that inexplicable thing
called 'presence.'"

That presence—that mysterious "it," as the star-making factor has been called in Hollywood since the days of silent movies—is hard enough to project on camera and usually doesn't translate into real life; when they step off the screen, most stars don't bring their Hollywood-magic charisma, or even their physical beauty, with them. To find "it" in a child, and both on and off screen at that, is exceedingly rare.

Badham was so struck by this quality that years later he suggested Jodie Foster as the female lead for a thriller he wanted to make from a soon-to-be published novel that he had the "first go at." The four motion picture studios he and his partner took the project to all turned it down, with one studio head saying, "Nobody wants to see a movie about skinning women. So I have no intention of making [*The*] *Silence of the Lambs*."

Eventually, after Badham and his partner failed to arouse studio interest, the rights to the novel were sold.

At the end of the first day of shooting the "Kung Fu" episode, Badham remembers, the state-mandated on-location teacher for Jodie had to be replaced because she didn't know enough French to instruct her precocious young pupil.

Unlike most other child actors, he says, Jodie's attention never wavered and she was never distracted by the long days, the tedium, or the take-after-take repetition.

She was always well-prepared and had thought through the meaning of her dialogue, says Badham, so that all the ten-year-old required from him were just "traffic-cop's directions—'stand over here,' 'walk in through that door,'" and so forth.

"She was just right there, just whatever was needed. . . . She had a quiet charisma, and it came through whether on-camera or off-camera. You felt like you were in the presence of an adult." That was precisely the quality that shone in her character in the TV story itself.

ATTRACTED BY HER mandolin playing, the itinerant monk Caine (David Carradine) discovers Alethea sitting on an outcropping above the road. She's dressed like a miniature adult, wearing a brown bonnet, tied with a big black bow under her determined chin, and a capelike coat over an ankle-length dress and clunky black shoes.

It's the typical kind of Sunday-goin'-to-prayer-meeting costume you've seen on God-fearing pioneer women in countless big- and small-screen oaters. But putting it on a child gives the costume a new and unexpected poignancy.

"Just practicing while I'm waiting for the stagecoach to take me into town," she tells him in her trademark husky voice—her matter-of-fact adult demeanor matching that tiny-adult outfit.

On cue the stagecoach arrives, and with it comes the TV narrative's preordained conflict: scurvy, belly-shootin' "road agents" intent on robbin' the stage.

As gunfire breaks out, Caine shields Alethea, who watches wide-eyed while a dying stagecoach driver throws Caine his gun—at the very same instant one of the robbers shoots the other coachman. To Alethea it appears that Caine has killed the man.

In timely TV fashion riders, led by the sheriff, who turns out to be Alethea's uncle, arrive to drive the road agents away Presently they take Caine, a suspicious stranger, into custody.

In flashback, in what series TV calls the *B-story*, the itinerant priest recalls as a child in a Chinese temple/monastery being taught the fable of the man who dreams he is a butterfly: the man wakes up and nevermore is certain if he's a man who dreamed he was a butterfly or a butterfly dreaming he is a man.

In the first of the many courtroom scenes throughout Foster's career, leading up to her Oscar-winning courtroom testimony in *The Accused*, Alethea takes the stand at Caine's trial and, despite her great affection for the priest, tells the truth as she perceived it: Caine is judged a killer, and he is sentenced to hang.

Later, when she comes to visit him in jail, Caine smilingly calls her "grasshopper," which, as all "Kung Fu" viewers know, is the young Caine's own Shaolin Temple nickname.

Caine fixes Alethea's mandolin, which was broken in the stage robbery, and, when he hands it back through the cell bars, asks her to play.

She takes it and in a clear voice, recorded live, begins to sing the Shaker hymn "Simple Gifts," made famous by Aaron Copland in *Appalachian Spring*.

It begins: " 'Tis a gift to be simple, 'tis a gift to be free, 'tis a gift to come down where we ought to be."

"She wasn't shy about singing it," director Badham remembers. "She didn't get weird the way some child actors do when you tell them they have to sing a solo."

As she sings and plays, she appears to be doing her own fingering on the instrument, although it's actually being played by a professional musician. Intercut with the song are shots of deputies hammering together the gallows in the town's square. Told what the noises are, Alethea stops playing and runs sobbing from the jail.

The next morning, at the very last instant, Alethea saves Caine from the noose, shouting "Stop it! I lied." (She didn't lie, of course, but this is, after all, series television, with all its time and other constraints.)

Finally, after the monk dispatches the real bad guys in the standard climactic fight scene, thus proving his innocence, Caine and Alethea have a brief but pointed talk about the difficulty of separating the truth from lies. Then, as little Alethea marches away down the town's dusty single street—and the camera pulls back and up into a panoramic overhead crane shot—we return to the B-story, in which the young Caine also has had his faith in adults sorely tested.

In the episode's final moments, back in the Shaolin Temple, the blind master asks the disillusioned little boy: "Your innocence, grasshopper, how shall that be returned?"

IT'S A QUESTION   that's vexed many a stage mom, too, since the first ringleted moppet vamped the first camera lens.

From "Paper Moon" on, one of Jodie Foster's most important recurring roles has been that of the seasoned trouper, out there for each new project (at first with her press agent mother, Brandy, then later very much alone), taking questions, posing for the photographers, and being profiled by the press.

Whether calculated or not, it's that kind of dutifulness that does not go unnoticed in executive suites.

After all, if you had the choice of hiring one of many talented and attractive young women, some of whom spent their time throwing tantrums, making demands, and partying in after-hours clubs, while one mostly stayed out of the tabloid spotlight and was smart enough to realize that promoting your product was good business for her too, whom would you choose?

The self-satisfied of show business are pleased to tell you that in Hollywood talent will always win out. Perhaps. But cooperation—getting with the program—goes a long way, too.

"I want to be president of the United States. I want to go on the stage. I want to go to Rome. And I want to get a hamster." Those were eleven-year-old Jodie Foster's "four ambitions," duly reported as part of the publicity drumbeat accompanying the premiere of "Paper Moon."[22]

Of course Rome happened, but first there was Hays, a little one-streetlight hamlet on the high plains of western Kansas, where her TV series went to shoot in the summer of 1974:

"I got to meet some nice kids my own age," the little trouper told *TV Guide* about her Kansas summer, adding that, because of her short haircut, the locals were constantly mistaking her for a little boy. "The only thing that bothers me is that everyone thinks I should look like Tatum O'Neal. One day Chris [Connelly, who played her con-man father] and I were playing Frisbee and I ran into the street after the Frisbee. An old farmer and his wife came by and started scolding Chris because he wasn't looking after his little boy better.

"But it's fun here. One day we missed a tornado by five minutes."[23]

On another day it was the wind of press agentry that was blowing extrahard: a straight-faced *TV Guide* writer allowed that a particularly stiff wind on an especially blustery day on location had nearly carried away Jodie's tiny Yorkshire terrier—a lovable yapper named Napoleon, after the character played by Johnnie Whitaker, her costar in *Napoleon and Samantha*, her first theatrical picture.

Says the same *TV Guide* article of the "incident": he was well on his way to Nebraska before an alert crew member made a midair grab of him.

Sure. It only looks like we're still in Kansas, Toto. Actually, what we've landed in is pure Hollywood.

The rules of promotion and publicity may not be precisely as immutable as, say, the laws of physics, but, then as now, in TV land the two most important times to get out there and beat the drums for a new series are as it premieres early in the fall season and during the November sweeps, when ratings are measured, both for the purposes of setting advertising rates and for making decisions about ordering additional episodes and renewing marginally rated but promising shows. Shows like "Paper Moon."

So, it should come as no surprise that, with her "Moon" being eclipsed by the formidably folksy "The Waltons" in the ratings, November of 1974 found one media-savvy preteen actress almost simultaneously charming a trade-paper columnist over lunch and getting surprisingly personal with *TV Guide*.

The bedazzzled columnist didn't exactly claim to have discovered Jodie Foster, modestly taking credit only for having "spotted Jodie a few years ago in a Crest Toothpaste commercial, and there was something special about her. . . . Jodie is a superb actress and an extremely bright 11-year-old."[24]

Interestingly enough, Foster, the PR-wise kid, leaves off praising her favorite TV shows ("M*A*S*H," "Maude," and "Multiplication Rock," which she called the "best thing on the air") to knock the western she was so effective on the year before:

"I don't really like 'Kung Fu,'" she declared. "It started out to be a peace show, but now all they do is karate and killing.

"I think violence on TV is bad for kids. It gives kids bad ideas, and I don't think it's necessary to the plot unless it's a documentary on the subject.

"I see a lot of things—I saw *Last Tango* in New York [i.e., *Last Tango in Paris*, a landmark film about sex and obsession, starring Marlon Brando and Maria Schneider and directed by Bernardo Bertolucci]. It didn't bother me. Just the violence does."

An eleven-year-old's bravado aside, remarks like that must have raised eyebrows among parents whose children weren't wised-up show business professionals.

"People think they fall apart, are ruined for life," said Brandy Foster, implicitly replying to such criticism in a *TV Guide* article. "Well, I don't think Elizabeth Taylor, Jackie Cooper, Shirley Temple or most of the others who have grown up in the business bear out any of that doom-saying."

Notes the writer, Terry Galanoy, in a snippy but to-the-point aside: "Mention of Judy Garland was politely avoided."

Six years later, as if replying to that sort of criticism and defending her mother, who then was still guiding her daughter's career, seventeen-year-old Jodie Foster made this clear distinction:

"I don't think it's child actors who have problems. . . . It's the children of actors who have it the roughest. That Malibu, Beverly Hills, La Scala [a popular restaurant with a power-lunching clientele] scene can be vicious. If you're asked to understand it, but not be a part of it, it can be very confusing."[25]

But back in 1974 the November sweeps–timed *TV Guide* article, entitled "Raising Kid Stars for Fun and Profit," focused on Jodie and her mom, who had raised her children "without having a father around."[26]

Then as now, there could be no better way of raising viewers' consciousness of and interest in a failing series than a juicy article in their *TV Guide*. Its importance during the sweeps month of November can't be overestimated. Media-savvy Brandy must have known, as did the network and Paramount, the producing studio, that it probably was the last, best chance to save the show. Still, the piece's "hook"—the absentee father and the theory that in almost all of Jodie's TV and movie work, and certainly in "Paper Moon," the relationship between the little girl and the father figure was a "key" factor in the story—couldn't have been an easy one for Brandy Foster to swallow.

There are only two brief quotes in the entire article from the erstwhile subject herself, and one is surely made up or canned. (A canned quote is a prepared remark that most likely has been rehearsed and memorized; it might not be at all sincere, and it might not even originate with the speaker but may have first been written by a press agent or other celebrity handler.)

Here is the eleven-year-old's "list of specifications" for the ideal father:

"The ideal father," the reader can almost hear her recite, "would have the looks of Robert Redford, the sense of humor of Richard Harris [with whom she was then scheduled to do a picture] and the friendship of Chris Connelly [her costar]."

Years later the child-star charmer averred that she had been blissfully unaware of the high financial stakes or the responsibilities of the television business. In addition to all the guest-star appearances in the early and midseventies, she'd been a regular on both "Bob & Carol & Ted & Alice" and "The Courtship of Eddie's Father"; she'd costarred in, among other longer-form projects, *Smile, Jenny, You're Dead*, the pilot for the "Harry-O" detective series; and she'd starred in an Emmy-winning daytime special for young people, "Rookie of the Year," as well as in two other "ABC Afternoon Specials."

Her job, she had thought all along, was just to vamp the camera, and it had been fun. But for many of her kid-era peers, showbiz fun was in short supply. Their careers stalled, or they dropped out, or—like cute little Anissa Jones, who also was raised by a single mother and also had starred in a TV series ("Family Affair," with Johnnie Whitaker, Jodie Foster's first big-screen costar)—in their teens they ODed and died.

It was almost a decade before Jodie Foster returned to television, briefly, in a misbegotten movie of the week, titled *O'Hara's Wife*, a "trite little tale"[27] costarring Ed Asner as a businessman whose wife returns from the dead.

A gossip column item, in late 1980, suggested that Jodie had been lured back to the small screen to do *O'Hara's Wife* after her freshman year in college by the $200,000 salary, astronomical by early-eighties standards. Considering that tuition at her school, Yale, was around $9,000 per year at the time, it was, as various columnists noted, not a bad way to spend summer vacation.

Before that, also in 1980, she had been announced as the original lead in *The Best Little Girl in the World*, which became an acclaimed TV movie about anorexia nervosa. But after a visit by the producers to New Haven late in the year, a trade paper item suggested that "Jodie Foster is too healthy-looking to play the anorexia nervosa victim and will be replaced. . . . [The producers and Foster] agreed it would be too dangerous for the young thesp to lose 20 pounds (in a week?) to look like an anorexia victim."[28]

Inveterate Hollywood column readers understood that "too healthy-looking" phrase and the snide dig about losing twenty pounds "in a week"; in trade-column code it meant that she had gained too much weight while away at school. An item like that could start talk that would kill a career entirely.

With schadenfreude the preferred dish at any power-lunch restaurant, it wasn't unusual for chortling showbiz insiders to make deliciously gloomy career predictions. Usually, of course, they were right, too.

Film Roles

FROM HER VERY FIRST
big-screen picture on, young Jodie Foster got nary a discouraging word from the nation's big-league film critics—then as now a notoriously cold and capricious lot, as many a wounded actor or director will attest.

Of course, it may have helped that she was cute, blond, and blue-eyed, but there was that intelligence, too, always apparent in whatever she did and always separating her from the run-of-the-mill mob of adorable moppets perennially sprouting up around any Hollywood kids' casting call.

Jodie received a costarring credit in her first film, *Napoleon and Samantha*. The same year, she turned up in a much smaller role as well, billed as one of "K.C.'s Children" in *Kansas City Bomber*, according to most reviewers an above-average and effective MGM action picture, starring seventies sexpot Raquel Welch as the brawling but sensitive top hat in the killer world of roller derby—the K.C. Bomber herself.

In many ways *Napoleon and Samantha* was a typical Disney live-action family picture of the early seventies, the heartwarming story of a plucky little boy and an even pluckier little girl who "experience the hazards of nature" while "running away with a [circus] lion and crossing a mountain to stay with a recluse friend."[29]

The "recluse friend" was none other than Michael Douglas, then a rather gangling twenty-year-old, top-billed in this his fourth picture, and the eleven-year-old runaway boy was Johnnie Whitaker, a red-haired, freckle-faced, jug-eared kid who, after five years on TV's "Family Affair" sitcom, was already a pint-sized veteran.

If Jodie Foster's career in commercials began famously with a little dog nipping at her infant behind, her big-screen career began and almost ended—in an ironic bit of symmetry that was too good to be scripted—with a lion taking an impromptu, unscripted bite out of the same tender part of her anatomy.

A few years later, as a cocky teenager, Foster recalled the incident for Andy Warhol:

"There were two lions—one who was a stand-in, named Zambo, and another who was 25 years old, named Major, who had all his teeth out and couldn't do anything.

"It was really hot, like four o'clock in the afternoon, and you're not supposed to work lions after three. And Major wouldn't do [the shot], so they got Zambo to do it.

"Finally we got the shot. I was walking up the hill and the lion was behind me, being pulled by a piano wire—that was the only way they could get him to go. And I wasn't walking fast enough. He came around and bit me. I rolled down the hill."[30]

The lion trainer saved her, she told the flabbergasted pop artist, who at first made a flippant remark about no more sunburn commercials in *her* career. Then, somewhat daffily, he asked the teenager if she had a scar.

"A cute little dimple in the back," Foster replied. (Like the beauty mark on Marilyn Monroe's face, the location and description of the scar were details that changed with the telling and the teller. Sometimes, according to her mother, the lion's mark was on her hip; sometimes there were two bites, sometimes four puncture wounds—two on her front and two on her backside. In another account, the lion attacked after the day's shooting was over.) "I figured if I could get through that [lion attack], I could be an actress for life."[31]

Many years later, looking back on the lion attack that almost ended her film career before it began, Foster hazily recalled being immediately flown to a Portland, Oregon, hospital, where she was treated for the wounds. It was two weeks (or ten days, depending on the account) before she returned to the set. "My mom left it up to me," she said, when she was a twentysomething Oscar winner, "but I think she felt it was smarter for me to go back, you know, to get back on the horse that bucked me."[32]

A year after Zambo almost ate his then eight-year-old costar, little Johnnie Whitaker was Tom to Jodie's Becky Thatcher in the well-received two-and-a-half-million-dollar Reader's Digest/ United Artists coproduction of *Tom Sawyer*. The musical was the fourth film version of the Mark Twain classic. A year after that, they sang an appropriately adorable duet at the Academy Awards, doing "Love," one of the nominated songs, from Disney's animated *Robin Hood*.

As Samantha to little Johnnie's Napoleon, Jodie was "appealing," said *Daily Variety* in its inimitable and oft-burlesqued fashion, as the eleven-year-old hero's "femme playmate."[33]

Her Becky, said the trade paper, was "great," and *The Hollywood Reporter* enthused that she was "refreshing . . . she looks sweet but she's a very feisty kid."[34]

Then as now, cute kids with dramatic range weren't exempt from typecasting: In *One Little Indian*, another Disney family picture in which she had a featured part and twelfth billing (the western starred James Garner, with whom she would be reunited two decades later in the big-screen *Maverick*), she was already "her usual feisty self" as a widowed pioneer woman's daughter, "nowhere near the traditional Disney good little girl."[35]

IN THE 1973 PICTURE Garner is Clint Keyes, an army deserter on the run after trying to stop the destruction of an Indian encampment. Trekking with him across the New Mexico desert is Mark, a buckskin-clad, pidgin-speaking runaway boy who's been raised by the Cheyenne and, because this is a Disney picture, two lovable camels, Rosebud and her gangly baby, Thirsty.

Coming across an isolated ranch house in the wilds, Clint and Mark are taken in by a young mother (Vera Miles) and her daughter, Martha (Foster), who are preparing to leave the wilderness and move back to Colorado.

As she would so many other times in her career, Jodie again plays the independent-minded child of a single parent. The blue-eyed, flaxen-haired girl, herself as coltishly gangly as the baby camel, is dressed in bright yellow or blue, vaguely period, calico, but she's a distinctly modern presence:

She doesn't walk, she *saunters* or she *runs*. Her Martha speaks her mind, uncowed by adults or by little boys.

On her first glimpse of the great, cud-chewing Rosebud, Martha instantly wants to climb up there and have a ride. The little actress who'd been mauled by a lion in her first movie is utterly convincing in her enthusiasm for riding that camel; she even licks her lips in anticipation.

"Could I, could I ride it? *Please*?"

"You're a girl," protests the stoic lad raised by the Cheyenne, crossing his arms and turning away in disapproval.

"Well, she's the mother," replies Martha, quite sensibly, eyeing the huge, improbable-looking beast. "She's a girl, too."

Naturally, little Martha gets her way.

TWO DECADES LATER, after *Maverick*, Garner recalled the child actress as a "presence even then—such a little professional, she could do whatever needed to be done. . . . Her attitude and temperament haven't changed."[36]

Back then, though, the "feisty kid" was already a show business veteran. Here are her credits, as they appeared in Disney's production notes for *Napoleon and Samantha*:

"'My Three Sons,' 'Adam 12,' 'Julia,' 'Gunsmoke,' 'Daniel Boone,' 'Mayberry, R.F.D.,' and [she's] a semi-regular in 'The Courtship of Eddie's Father.'

"She has made about 45 commercials and was in the two-part show 'Menace on the Mountain' on the 'Wonderful World of Disney' TV anthology series several years ago.

"In her spare time, she composes and writes the lyrics for her songs, though she really wants to be a writer and loves reading history and historical novels. She is also fluent in French."

At the time of this rather breathless publicity department recitation, Jodie Foster had been her family's major breadwinner for more than a year and her mother had already become her full-time manager.

Jodie was four feet, five inches tall and weighed fifty-five pounds. She was just nine years old.

Just three years later, with the short-lived "Paper Moon" TV series already behind her, Jodie Foster was cast as Audrey in *Alice Doesn't Live Here Anymore*, a Warner Brothers picture directed by the acclaimed Martin Scorsese, then a hot young New York filmmaker, from Robert Getchell's script.

It was the kind of single-parent-with-bright-kid-who-has-adult-burdens story that would keep reappearing in Foster's career, only this time the focus was elsewhere: her character's single parent appeared in only one scene and she herself had only four, although Foster, eighth-billed in the credits, came near to stealing the picture.

IN HER OSCAR-WINNING ROLE, Ellen Burstyn stars as Alice, who heads west with her son Tommy (Alfred Lutter) just as soon as her loutish trucker husband dies in a car crash. They stop in Phoenix, where Alice pursues her girl-hood dream of becoming a singer, but an abusive, violent boyfriend (Harvey Keitel), who also turns out to be married, forces Alice and Tommy to escape to Tucson, where Alice is reduced to working as a waitress at Mel and Ruby's Café, which is populated by various charming eccentrics, including another would-be beau (Kris Kristofferson). (This part of the picture was the basis for the long-running "Alice" TV series, in which such pungent film dialogue as "Give yourself a jack job in a paper sack" was dumbed down to the trademark "Kiss my grits.")

In Tucson, Alice's bored eleven-year-old son takes guitar lessons, outside of which he meets the self-named Audrey (Foster)—"It's really Doris, but I like Audrey better"—an androgynous, bony limbed kid in jeans and T-shirt who informs him that "Tucson is the weird capital of the world," adding casually that "Dad split two years ago, [and] Mom turns tricks at the Ramada Inn from three on in the afternoon."

Audrey, a thin, narrow-eyed waif with a unisex shag haircut, is another of Foster's wised-up, totally contemporary girls. None of them lives in the traditional "Leave It to Beaver" two-parent family, and every one of them is hip and hardened.

Like all her cinematic sisters incarnated by the young, naturalistic kid actress, Audrey knows all about the adult world and its dangerous hypocrisies.

"Wanna get high on Ripple?" she asks in the film's single most famous line, cracking to the amazed Tommy that "I could have a troop of bare-assed Eagle Scouts at four in the afternoon, and [Mom] wouldn't even notice."

Later she teaches Tommy, who needs guitar strings, to shoplift. Followed into the local music store by Scorsese's handheld camera, Audrey throws herself to the floor in front of a sales clerk as a diversion, pointing to a "slick spot" and grabbing her knee in mock pain, saying dryly, "I hope this doesn't ruin my tryout for cheerleader."

Late in the picture, when she and Tommy finally get drunk on cheap wine, Audrey reminisces about her absent parent: "My dad was a bastard all right," she says, with a hint of a slur. "He used to make me bend over while he whipped me with his belt."

The two kids wind up at a police station, hung over and caught trying to shoplift. When Alice shows up to get Tommy, Audrey sticks out her hand in forthright greeting, while the handheld camera circles the scene. "So you're the singing waitress," she says.

Her last line in the picture sums up the tough little girl's world-view. As her mom yanks her out the police station door, she calls out, "So long, suckers!"

AT THE AUDITION to cast the role of Audrey, Scorsese recalled, "in came this little girl with a Lauren Bacall voice. . . . She cracked us up."[37]

The wine-guzzling preteen cracked up audiences, too—and, because of the short "Paper Moon" haircut that gave her a boyish look and that "Ripple" line, confused and scandalized some as well. But it marked the beginning of Jodie Foster's transformation from cute kid to teenager and led directly to her most controversial role.

THE TAXI DRIVER
AND THE
LITTLE GIRL

FILM IS JUST ANOTHER
business, she would insist all throughout her blasé teen-sophisticate years, and acting is just another job.

"People ask me what it was like playing a 13-year-old prostitute," she remarked as a seventeen-year-old, less than a year away from college.

"I wasn't playing a prostitute in *Taxi Driver*. I was playing a runaway. I don't go for that 'get-into-the-role' stuff.

"I'm a technician, like any other crew member. I do my job and the electrician does his. What I'm good at is making eyes at the camera."[1]

To the present day, Jodie Foster has continued that commendable emphasis on the multifaceted craft of filmmaking. Truly, acting is just one among many of its integral parts, as even a cursory visit to a bustling film set, the noisy dream-factory floor employing upward of 150 craftspeople and technicians, will show. But

Jodie was to learn, in a way more dramatic than any fiction writer could imagine, that to some people acting is more than just another job, that a film can change lives, and that out there, in the darkened theater, are some in the audience who confuse the image and the image maker.

Still, even after a deranged Travis Bickle manqué had shot four men, including the president of the United States, claiming he was just trying to win her love and respect with a "historical deed," Foster's initial public pose was to claim that "how much film-making had to do with any of this has been purely a figment of the media's imagination."[2]

TAXI DRIVER, directed by Martin Scorsese from Paul Schrader's original script, is a great American film in which all the craft elements have come powerfully and transcendently together, from the acting to the expressive Bernard Herrmann score.

The 1976 Columbia Pictures film stars Robert De Niro as Travis Bickle, the taxi driver of the title, prowling the streets of a neon-smeared night-world New York City in a yellow Checker cab (photographed by cinematographer Michael Chapman like some sleek, stalking predator) and seething with inchoate rage.

The loner ex-marine cabbie, living in solitary squalor, unable to sleep, is both disgusted by and drawn to the depravity of the mean streets. Subsisting on junk food and popping pills, spurned by Betsy (Cybill Shepherd), a volunteer in a presidential campaign who is the most beautiful woman he's ever seen, Travis Bickle comes unhinged, arming himself for (paradoxically apolitical) political violence. In the bicentennial year the film was widely taken as stylized social commentary.

"GET ME OUTTA HERE, all right?" The teen hooker (Foster) in tight hot pants and halter top has hopped into the back of Bickle's cab. Her pimp (Harvey Keitel) pulls her out roughly, dismissively throws a crumpled-up bill on the front seat, and tells the taxi driver just to forget about it.

But the taxi driver can't forget, and that night, on his first date with Betsy, he takes her to a hard-core porn movie, revolting her.

Rejected, Bickle spirals down toward his own inevitable Götterdämmerung, transferring his obsession from the madonnalike Betsy to Iris, the preteen whore.

"You lookin' for some action?" When he approaches her on a daylit street, she sizes him up immediately, directing him to her pimp in a nearby doorway.

Fifteen dollars for fifteen minutes, twenty-five for half an hour, says Matthew, the pimp Iris calls Sport. "Take it or leave it. If you wanna save yourself some money, don't fuck her, 'cause you'll be back here every night for some more, man. She's twelve-and-a-half-years old. . . ."

The jittery pimp's brief and brutal litany of possible violations, practically a compendium of what we've now learned to call "unsafe sex," ends with an ironic admonition: "But no rough stuff."

Nonchalantly the girl leads the taxi driver into a room in a seedy by-the-hour hotel next door, where she lights a cigarette, balances it in an ashtray, and tells him that when the cigarette has burned out his time will be up.

As she sits down and starts to take off her shoes, Bickle asks her name.

"Easy," she replies. An easy name to remember. Besides, she adds with a grimace, "I don't like my real name . . . Iris."

Viewed by the camera from behind, she begins to slip off her blouse. "How'd you wanna make it?" she asks matter-of-factly, standing up.

She runs her hand down his arm. "Wanna make it like this?" she asks, unhooking his belt.

The camera cuts to her upturned face; we hear the sound of his zipper being pulled down.

But the taxi driver is there to save her, he tells her, zipping back up and fastening his belt. He reminds her of the day she jumped in his cab; she doesn't remember him, it was of no consequence, she must've been stoned.

"I can help you," she says, dropping to her knees in front of him. She reaches toward him; again, we hear his zipper going down. The taxi driver pushes her away.

He just wants to take her out, buy her a meal, talk. OK, she says, breakfast at one o'clock tomorrow.

When they get together in the bright daylight, it's not the teen hooker who shows up, but an all-American girl who might be right out of the Disney movies—long straight blond hair, neatly parted, a pink T-shirt and bell-bottoms, her guileless, girlish blue eyes at first behind green shades, which she takes off, then exchanges for another pair, blue this time.

She piles jelly and sugar on her toast, says she wants to go live in a commune, and prattles on about astrological signs. "You're a Scorpio," says Iris, skipping lightly right over the taxi driver's dangerous intensity. "I can tell every time."

She giggles girlishly. "Are you a narc?" she asks abruptly. Yes, the taxi driver agrees. "Gawd," she says, "I don't know who's weirder, you or me."

Later, we see Iris back in her dimly lighted room with Sport, telling him with a note of desperation in her voice that she doesn't like what she's doing. The pimp calms and reassures her with whispered endearments, and we see them slow dancing.

With her head on Sport's chest, her arms wrapped tightly around his waist, Iris, childlike, has her eyes closed while Sport gently strokes her golden hair, telling her how much he loves her.

Later the taxi driver returns, killing the pimp and the other men who've been using the barely teenage girl.

In a chilling coda to the blood-soaked finale, we learn that society has misconstrued the maniac, making Travis Bickle a hero, and that he may have really done some good, saving Iris from her life on the streets.

In voice-over narration, as the camera pans laudatory news clippings covering Travis Bickle's once-barren apartment wall, we hear a letter from Iris's grateful father, Mister Burt Steensma of

Pittsburgh, Pennsylvania, thanking the taxi driver on behalf of himself and his wife, Ivy, and informing him that Iris is back in school and working hard.

SCHRADER, THE SCREENWRITER, blithely maintained that the movie went right over the head of the thirteen-year-old actress, which, particularly after the picture's publicity campaign was over and the furor had died down, she steadfastly denied.

It was around that time that film critic Roger Ebert first met the young actress, and she was anything but an oblivious naïf. "She was so together for such a young person," he recalls. "I was going to interview her [in Los Angeles] and she said, Let's meet at the Old World restaurant on the [Sunset] Strip [which at the time was a trendy health-food restaurant].

"She came by herself—no agent, no publicist, no mother, just Jodie. Then later on, at the Cannes Film Festival, I remember the press conference after the movie. She acted as the translator for Scorsese, De Niro, Keitel; you know, putting everything into and out of French for everybody. And I thought to myself, this is an extraordinary person."

"When I did *Taxi Driver*," she said five years later, "it was the first time I ever did a role that was a little out of character. I felt when I came home that I'd really accomplished something. We were working improvisation—half the film was improvised. And for the first time, I saw a real technique, a real style."[3]

That technique came not from her director, Foster said more than a decade after making the picture, but from her costar: "For some reason [Scorsese] never gave me any direction. He didn't have much to do with my performance. . . . Actually, De Niro did. He didn't tell me to do things, but he rehearsed with me over and over, and I knew the script so well that when we started shooting and he threw improvs at me, it was no problem."[4]

Although their coffee shop scene, for example, was so naturalistic as to seem overheard, "there wasn't one spontaneous thing about it," Foster recalled a decade later. "The scene we shot in the coffee shop was rehearsed for one straight week. I could recite it in my sleep. We did an entire day of one master—fifty or so takes—yet it looks very spontaneous and intuitive."[5]

A newsweekly had described her then, at age thirteen, as "neither a button-nosed naïf like the young Hayley Mills, nor a hard-edged precocious, like Tatum O'Neal. . . .

"She does not date, or attend Hollywood functions. She is disarmingly unconcerned about money. Aside from the $1,600 in a savings account from her dollar-a-week allowance, 'a few bets' and 'liars' poker with the movie crews,' she has no idea how much her manager-mother has stashed away. 'After all,' says Jodie. 'I'm just a kid.'"[6]

The dollar-per-week allowance is a nice touch, but notice that the "disarmingly unconcerned" child star would actually have to be a thirty-year-old midget and have been thriftily stashing away dollar bills since her birth to have saved up that kind of money. Either that or she was a precocious poker shark, and *she* should have gotten the *Maverick* title role.

While the press couldn't help noticing that The Kid was growing up, that she was now a leggy teen who had given up her childhood ambition of being president or of joining the navy or of maybe becoming a lawyer, and that she now declared firmly that she wanted to practice her acting craft seriously—"I'm an actress who happens to play children's roles"[7]—the post–*Taxi Driver* publicity spin returned again and again to her innocence.

"I never feel like the people I'm playing," she told *Time*, and her mother added: "I couldn't believe how she looked in her [hooker] wardrobe. Suddenly she had legs. I don't think I'd ever seen her with her hair curled. I was very happy when she returned to her grubby little self."

Given her utterly convincing portrayal of a seen-it-all, done-it-all teen hooker in Scorsese's prophetic urban nightmare, the spin wasn't surprising. Even before the film was screened, letters to the editor from concerned parents around the country were protesting her alleged exploitation.

Before the Los Angeles Welfare Board even allowed her to play the part, a UCLA psychiatrist had to certify, after a four-hour interview, that her morals wouldn't be undermined.

"I suppose they figured that if I was willing to play a part like that, I had to be insane," Jodie deadpanned in the *Time* profile.

And of the legal battle that preceded the shooting, in which former California governor Edmund "Pat" Brown was enlisted to argue her case, Brandy Foster declared that she was "determined to win. Here was some board trying to tell me what was too adult for my own daughter."[8]

As the former governor recalled it, Columbia, the producing studio, "ran into real difficulties with the state Department of Labor. That was a pretty rough script."[9] So they asked Brown to intercede, but he insisted the studio send their precocious child actress to the UCLA psychiatrist first. "He found she has a very high I.Q. . . . and he told me the script wouldn't hurt her. Based on that, I took the case."

Even after the psychiatrist signed off on the role, though, the board stipulated that a scene in which she unbuttoned her blouse while facing the camera would have to be cut and that other sexually explicit scenes would be filmed with a body double—who turned out to be Jodie's twenty-one-year-old sister Connie. However, those scenes, including one in which Connie-as-Iris unzips Travis Bickle, ended up on the cutting room floor.[10]

Although *Time* magazine and others at the time had Foster preparing for her role by spending a month of her summer vacation dolled up in her Iris character's hot pants and six-inch platform shoes and walking the streets of the Lower East Side, even noting, somewhat incredibly, that she was never picked up, Foster herself demurred: "It was all untrue. . . . I had two guards with me the whole time. . . . They did bring a real hooker along to location one day, but she was no help. She just talked in clichés."[11]

"I'd like to say I studied and concentrated and researched," she said on another occasion, "and that it all just came out of me. But I'm not a method actor. . . . I've never been [a hooker]. And I've never observed or talked to a teen-age prostitute.

"But listen, kids aren't stupid anymore, like they used to be. Everybody knows what hookers are. You see them in movies and on TV, you see them on Hollywood Boulevard. All the kids know how they act."[12]

However hard it may be to suspend disbelief when it comes to some of the more disingenuous comments made for and by the thirteen-year-old, the remark is an understandable response to a risky role that could have backfired.

Two years before, she'd condemned the mild, stylized TV violence on "Kung Fu," but now, assaying the new role of hip teenager, she could say of *Taxi Driver*'s explicit killing spree: "The violence was fun. It was my favorite part. I know it brought the film down a little bit, but I think it helped my acting. If I had seen the film first, I would have been shocked. The only thing that bothered me was the smell of blood."[13] (Of course, whatever the smell was that bothered her, it wouldn't have been actual blood. Among its other drawbacks, real blood doesn't photograph properly, and substitutes have been in wide use at least since the dawn of color films.)

Scorsese, De Niro, Foster: serious cinematic artists undertaking a serious theme. To her cinema-savvy single mother, steeped in the countercultural currents of those days, the risky role must have seemed well worth taking on, despite the certainty of criticism.

Indeed Iris catapulted the young performer from the Disney stable to the front rank of American actresses and earned her an Oscar nomination as well as critical recognition from, among others, the Los Angeles Film Critics Association, then a new organization, which bestowed on her and Scorsese its first-ever New Generation Awards. But insisting that she was still just The Kid, that she hadn't been shocked or even affected by playing the role, must have seemed a necessary and soothing corrective for young

Jodie's legions of fans, who knew her only from Disney pictures and saccharine TV sitcoms. And the spin was based on one undeniable fact: Jodie Foster was on the cusp between goofy-kid-dom and sophisticated young womanhood. Growing up in public, she could, almost simultaneously, sound like both.

The controversy over her *Taxi Driver* role was hard to overlook, but ultimately it took a backseat to her acting, which was almost uniformly praised and resulted in the Best Supporting Actress nomination. In one of that year's biggest surprises, though, the Oscar went to Beatrice Straight for her brief portrayal of the wife William Holden spurns for Faye Dunaway in *Network*.

Looking ahead to that year's Oscars, the teenage Foster was sanguine—and savvy—about her prospects: "There are so many grown-up actresses working for so long who've never gotten an award; it doesn't seem right to give one to a kid," she said, paying proper respect to both her elders and to the bottom line. "I hate to sound like a business person, but if I did get an award, that would mean I could make more money, because the awards are really a way to get your price higher."[14]

With greater visibility came adult-sized expectations . . . and disputes. In the show business trade papers her mother rattled the litigation saber (unsuccessfully) to prevent a British filmmaker from dubbing her singing voice in *Bugsy Malone*.

Rumors spread that, post-*Taxi*, she was "difficult" on the set of *The Little Girl Who Lives Down the Lane*.

That 1976 picture, much maligned but little seen, in many ways was just as much a challenge and a testament to Jodie Foster's uncanny acting ability as was *Taxi Driver*. Perhaps more so. Foster was top billed and in every scene.

The movie, a Canadian-French coproduction that was released in the United States by American International Pictures, a company best known for drive-in shlock, is often characterized as a horror picture; actually, it's a moody psychological suspense thriller that depends for verisimilitude entirely on Jodie Foster's performance as thirteen-year-old Rynn Jacobs, the title role.

IS WINTRY-EYED RYNN, her long blond hair cut in a midseventies straight-bangs-and-flip style, reminiscent of Julie Christie, a killer child? Why is she always alone in her house, and where is her poet father? Her landlady, the imperious and anti-Semitic Mrs. Hallet (Alexis Smith) demands to know the father's whereabouts; she isn't used to being put in her place by a little girl, and she's determined to get back at Rynn. You have a mocking tone and hurt eyes, Mrs. Hallet tells Rynn accusingly. Hallet's son Frank (Martin Sheen), a child molester under his mother's autocratic protection, has his own designs on the pretty, solemn little girl in the house at the end of the lane.

"How old do you have to be before people start treating you like an adult, huh?" Rynn asks Mario (Scott Jacoby), a crippled older boy from the nearby village of Wells Harbor she befriends and in whom she confides.

Her dying poet father wanted her to be on her own, she finally explains to Mario, and before his death he arranged the three-year house rental and a cache of traveler's checks for her. "'Fight them any way you have to. Survive.' That's what he said," she tells the boy.

At the story's end, with her last tormentor dying in front of her and Chopin's *Piano Concerto No. 1 in E Minor* playing on the soundtrack, the camera slowly pushes in to an extreme close-up of Rynn's impassive face while, in the background fireplace, flames blaze yellow as her hair.

"I DID WALK OFF the [*Little Girl*] set," Foster conceded to an interviewer two years later. The problem was a nude scene—in the picture a shot of Rynn's bare torso viewed from the back—that eventually was "doubled" by Jodie's older sister, Connie. "It wasn't temperament; it was the straw that broke the camel's back. In the first place, this crazy producer kept saying he wanted me to pull my dress lower. I decided he was nuts. I used to tell him to shut up. He really was an idiot. Everyone hated him.

"Finally, one day he said, 'We have to have sex and violence or the picture won't sell.' So I said, 'Well, I'm not going to get into that.' A couple of weeks later, I was told they were doing the scene, and I wasn't in it. I talked to the producer and got emotional and started to cry because, well, I'm young, so I cry. And I walked off. I was really upset."[15]

By mid-1976, young Jodie Foster, the thirteen-year-old who could speak fluent French, was the surprise hit of the Cannes Film Festival, where no fewer than three of her films were being screened—*Bugsy Malone*, the all-kid roaring-twenties musical crime spoof, directed by Alan Parker, that was Britain's official entry; *The Little Girl Who Lives Down the Lane*; and *Taxi Driver*, which won the Grand Prix.

"Accompanied by her mother, she ran the testing course of interviews, photo calls and parties with a polite and amused calm that also wowed the journalists who have had an unusual run this time of adult stars who wouldn't talk if they had lighted matches under their fingernails or who have answered with supercilious contempt," said one critic. "The feeling is that Jodie will be returning to Cannes long after she has graduated from high school."[16] (In fact, she was back in the French seaside city the very next year, stopping in at another Cannes festival, where, once again, the French-speaking teenager was a "popular figure particularly with radio and TV."[17])

Just turned fourteen and beginning the second decade of her professional career, Jodie Foster was undeniably a movie star.

She was even bright enough and famous enough to host "Saturday Night Live," in her first live performance, which at the time she called "weird but fun."

It was as good a description as any of the mood of the country, right after the election of Jimmy Carter, midway through the anything-goes, "liberated" seventies. The media myth of flower power and the hippies may have begun to wane at Altamont, at the end of the swinging sixties, but sex, drugs, and rock and roll still were everywhere.

In California Patty Hearst had just been sentenced to jail, in Utah Gary Gilmore had just demanded the state carry out his death penalty, and in China Mao Tse-tung had just died (his widow was immediately arrested). In New York on November 27, 1976, Foster was performing with the original SNL cast—Aykroyd, Belushi, Radner, and the rest—in sketches, such as kinky "Mister Mike's Least-Loved Bedtime Tales," that still were stretching the bounds of what was acceptable, even on not-ready-for-prime-time network TV.

IN ONE SKETCH she introduces an amazing new product called Puberty Helper, a gigantic body-covering brown bag with cutout eyeholes and an appliquéd happy face, by facing the camera and saying:

"Hi, I'm Jodie Foster, and if you're like me, you're going through those awkward years between thirteen and eighteen, when everything seems wrong.

"Believe me," she continues with actorly sincerity, "as cute as I am, I know how it is to hate your body and wish you could trade it in for somebody else's. That's why I'm glad I discovered Puberty Helper . . . So why not try it before it's too late and you find out how lame you are?"

Then while she struggles into one of the huge bags, Dan Aykroyd does his fast-talking pitchman routine, touting the Puberty Helper as good for everything from zits to pregnancy, and available by mail order for $49.95 from Loss Leader, New Jersey.

But the most memorable sketch featured Foster as Wendy and Laraine Newman and John Belushi, in their yellow-and-black bee costumes, as Peter and Tinkerbee.

It begins with Foster, a typical midseventies teen in a green

Peter Frampton sweatshirt and jeans, kneeling on her bed in her room, talking on the telephone. Big padded headphones are around her neck. Naturally the subject is rock and roll.

"Oh, right, yeah, man," she's saying in a nasal, spacy-Val voice. "I mean Pink Floyd, this really great group from the sixties, they're really hot.

"No, listen, Aerosmith is loud, but you can't hold loudness against them. . . ."

That established, she hangs up and slips the headphones over her ears, and a xylophone tinkles as Newman and Belushi leap mock-heroically through the window, bouncing onto the bed behind her.

"Wendy," Newman calls out in fairy-tale singsong.

As Foster takes off the headphones, her face and intonation go doper-slack and boggled. "Hey," she expostulates, "I knew I was wrecked, but not this wrecked."

"Wendy, I'm Peter, and this is Tinkerbee," trills Newman, "and we've come to take you off to the Land of the Lost Bees—"

Putting her hand to her face in disbelief, Foster interjects, "I've been wrecked before, but I've handled it, you know."

"Where you never grow up," Newman concludes.

"Yeah," reiterates Foster, with a druggy weight, "I mean, I've been through a lot of heavy stuff, but I've handled it."

"You could learn to fly, too!"

"Oh, listen, I mean something like this happened to me at a Dead concert once, but it lasted two hours, hour-and-a-half tops."

"Wendy," tsks Newman disapprovingly, "I sense you don't believe me."

At the edge of the scene Belushi is reacting to Wendy's disbelief by turning red-faced, gurgling, and squirming: Tinkerbee, on cue, is dying of disbelief.

"Yeah," says Foster, "you're bees, and I'm Bianca Jagger, and I carry a cane for no known reason. . . ."

The audience titters at this joke à la mode while Belushi thrashes around.

"Let's face it, you're not bees. You're actors—"

More squirming and flailing.

"You're television actors. I've seen you. You're OK when you get a good concept."

Belushi falls off the bed, kicking out in extremis on the floor.

"You're killing him!" Newman wails.

"Hey," shrugs Foster, "y'know I'm really sorry, but listen: it's the seventies. Y'know, the seventies: Frye boots, yogurt—frozen yogurt, uh-huh—'Goodbye Yellow Brick Road.' I mean, kids are different now. We don't believe in bees."

THE YOUNG PRO proclaimed herself unfazed by the live telecast, saying she was nervous only during the dress rehearsal because "it's very weird. Nobody claps, and at the bad things they boo."[18]

These may be virtually the only boos that the young, universally acclaimed actress heard. The good reviews kept coming, even for a high-concept musical pastiche in which her own distinctive voice was dubbed by a Betty Boop–sounding adult.

Bugsy Malone was British commercial director–turned–filmmaker Alan Parker's first film. Looking back at it fifteen years later, he winced watching the talented teenager doing one of her speakeasy numbers. "Jodie Foster is miming to a rather strange adult voice," he conceded drolly. "I didn't know she was going to be famous; if I had, I would've used her own voice."[19]

Clearly, though, she already was famous. At that point in her career, she certainly didn't need to go back to Disney to shoot two of its high-concept family pictures, with a mere three weeks between the two films. But she did, for a two-picture deal, making *Freaky Friday* in California and *Candleshoe* on location in England.

Of the two, *Candleshoe* is the more interesting picture. In *Freaky Friday*, based on a novel by Mary Rodgers, she was cast as a girl whose wish to change places with her mother, played by Barbara Harris, comes true, and in *Candleshoe*, based on the Michel Innes book, she played a tough Los Angeles waif posing as the long-lost granddaughter of a wealthy British dowager.

While hardly *Great Expectations* or *Oliver Twist*, *Candleshoe* did surround the young Foster with such expert players as venerated first lady of the stage Helen Hayes, suave David Niven, and ubiquitous, basso profundo–voiced Leo McKern—some of that time's best-known acting names.

By the time of *Candleshoe*, Foster, at fourteen, was the very epitome of the nonchalant teen sophisticate. "I don't feel comfortable working with children," she said airily, and less than gallantly, before going off to join a cast that included four other kids.[20]

(Looking back on it all from the vantage point of young adulthood, she admitted that "when I was young, nobody ever called me on anything. Nobody ever busted my chops about anything I said. They humored me, I suppose, because they only had to put up with me for about a month."[21])

Her teen bravado was seasoned by the voice of experience, however; of child stars in the thirties and forties, for example, she said dismissively that "those old Hollywood kids never really had to act. All they did was look cute, love Mummy and Daddy, and hug Lassie or their horse. Shirley Temple was never an actress!"[22]

At about the same age, Helen Hayes had been at the very beginning of her long and honored career.

"Of course there are pressures when you're so young," Hayes said during the *Candleshoe* shoot. "[Jodie] likes to pretend she has no nerves. But when we started the film, I thought I detected that she was a bit tightly strung. So I told her I was nervous, and she confessed that she was nervous, too!"[23]

WITH HER BLOND HAIR in a shoulder-length shag perpetually falling Veronica Lake–ish into her eyes, Jodie is Casey Brown, a pink-cheeked teenage cynic with a spray of freckles and a boyish swagger (an obvious cousin to her Audrey from *Alice*

Doesn't Live Here Anymore), an orphan in a khaki army shirt with cut-off sleeves and bell-bottom jeans, toughened by Los Angeles street life and a succession of uncaring foster parents in it just for the welfare payments.

"The whole world's a racket's the first thing I ever learned," she sneers, running a hand through her hair.

"Casey Brown: no parents, no memory of home," bellows the mysterious Brit (McKern) who's snatched her up. "Apparent age, fourteen. Character, bellicose. Four times remanded to juvenile hall, one time committed to correctional facility."

To which curriculum vitae little Casey replies: "I ain't deprived; I'm delinquent. There's a difference, you know."

He's Harry Bundage, a low-life would-be Fagin with a dastardly scheme: take the girl to England where she will impersonate the long-lost granddaughter of Lady St. Edmund (Hayes), who lives in baronial splendor in the grand manor house called Candleshoe, near the picturesque village of Compton-in-the-Hole in Warwickshire.

But because this is a live-action Disney movie of the midseventies, that long period of drought between the death of the founder and the revival of the studio by those Wall Street darlings Michael Eisner and Jeffrey Katzenberg, the so-called (and now defunct) Team Disney, that promising setup soon gives way to a treasure hunt for the pirate's gold hidden at Candleshoe by her ladyship's ancestor.

David Niven, who spent a career cast as an aristocrat, is below stairs in this one as Priory, the butler, who impersonates the Irish gardener and the cockney chauffeur, among others, to keep from Lady St. Edmund the dire financial straits into which Candleshoe has fallen.

Throw in the four local foster children living at Candleshoe, and a tax bill that must be paid or else Lady St. Edmund will be forced to quit the ancestral seat, and all that's left of the original premise is a scene or two between Hayes and Foster, when the tough young orphan's bravado—"I ain't alone. I got me"—gives way to affection for the aristocratic grande dame.

"I came here to do a straight hustle on you . . . but now it's different," she sniffs, on the verge of tears. In a touching moment Niven and Hayes waltz to a gramophone record in the empty grand ballroom, and Lady St. Edmund reveals that she's been aware of her butler's deception.

"We were playing games with time, you and I," the great stage actress says, "and I am grateful for it."

OF COURSE, once again Jodie Foster received glowing reviews for what were after all minor films—reviews that often saluted her rare ability to convey intelligence as an actress and empathetic qualities like "knowingness" and "contemporary authenticity" as a public young person.

Reviews aside, returning to Disney after playing Iris in *Taxi Driver* was a smart career move—it showed range and underlined her acting ability, as well as demonstrated loyalty to the studio where she'd made her first film. And in Hollywood, with its club rules and old boys' traditions, showing loyalty and respect is always a smart move.

EUROTEEN/
VALLEY GIRL

WHILE MIDDLEBROW
American audiences were watching Jodie Foster play the appealing tomboy again in her two final Disney movies, Eurofilm fans were seeing her lose her on-screen virginity. Of course, it happened demurely, "sans sex scenes, with her usually waking up the morning after, chastely covered after an embrace."[1]

The picture was *Moi, Fleur Bleue* (*Me, Blue Flower*), known also in the American art houses where it played briefly as *Stop Calling Me Baby!* In it, she was cast as a fourteen-year-old "rough-talking girl with the heart and body of a virgin."[2] American expatriate actress Sydne Rome costarred as her older sister. Jodie Foster was just fifteen, and during the shooting she lived in a Paris apartment with her mother.

Meanwhile, a few entertainment writers, while noting her enormous wholesome appeal, had taken to expressing a vague puzzlement, calling her, for example, "one of the more mysterious young actresses in Hollywood."[3] Were comments like this veiled references to her sexuality? It's impossible to know for certain, and that's exactly the point. Reading between the lines is very common practice in Hollywood, where showbiz players regularly signal each other with planted stories in the trade papers and industry gossip columns thrive on wink-wink, nudge-nudge items that are often meaningless to a general reader. Entertainment-beat writers, who regularly hear stories unproved but widely assumed to be true, often make these kind of mysterious-young-actresses references, passing by general readers but drawing knowing smiles from the gossiping cognoscenti.

To most of her fans, though—those who wrote her, care of the Magic Kingdom, by the thousands—she remained the embodiment of the modern American girl: intelligent, independent, in control. "I'm treated as an adult now and have been for a long time," she told an American gossip columnist[4] from Paris, where she was cutting a single of a ballad, called in English "When I Look at Your Face," for a French record company and looping her own French dialogue for *Moi, Fleur Bleue* (the first American actress, the publicists trumpeted, since Jane Fonda to loop her own French-language dialogue).

She didn't yet date, she added, "not because of any rules that have been set down, but because it doesn't interest me at this point in my life." It was a theme that was repeated over the next few years.

But not everyone stayed on message. For example, during the period leading up to the premiere of *Foxes* almost two years later, while Jodie herself was still telling one magazine that she had no plans to marry, that she wasn't "mature enough to be nice to anyone else," and that she liked best "being alone" in her room with a stack of books,[5] her mother was telling another magazine that her daughter dated a couple of times a week, confiding that "she has a weakness for small, dark men."[6]

Her Paris summer spent shooting *Moi, Fleur Bleue* followed the Italian filming of *Il Casotto* (also known in the United States, where it played briefly in 1980, as *The Beach*, *The Beach House*, and *Beach Bungalow*) and was presented by one newsmagazine as an all-American idyll:

Youthful Jodie was out "exploring Parisian streets on a motorcycle, skateboarding under the Eiffel Tower, fishing from a bank of the Seine, flying a kite and tossing a Frisbee on the Ile St. Louis."[7]

(In reality, as she told one interviewer, she hated motorcycles and allowed a photographer to snap her on one only for publicity purposes.)

Meanwhile, art house, European, and "international" filmgoers were able to catch Foster the grown-up Eurostarlet, brightening otherwise misbegotten cult pictures, at least one of which reviewers labeled "soft core"—portentous pictures presumably more attuned to the febrile, do-it-if-it-feels-good, disco-til–you-drop world that kids her own age inhabited in the pre-AIDS late seventies.

Il Casotto, for example, was the first feature directed by Sergio Citti, who learned his craft as an assistant director on many of Pier Paolo Pasolini's films. Pasolini, a habitué of Rome's sex-and-drugs gay-street-hustler demimonde who was later murdered in that milieu, was known for films that shocked the bourgeoisie with anticlerical, homoerotic, or sadomasochistic subject matter (*The Canterbury Tales*, *The Decameron*).

The picture, in which Foster costarred with Catherine Deneuve, one of the great beauties of the European cinema, was meant to be a kind of farcical beach-house-of-fools, with an aggregation of Italian city dwellers converging on a public beach house outside Rome to play out their various, mostly sexual fantasies. Intoned the bible of show business of the "near sexpo":

"Little of the farce works. . . . Catherine Deneuve is wasted in an absurd dream sequence, while Jodie Foster, as a pregnant teen whose grandparents scheme to find her a husband, has little to do but thrust out her chest."[8]

As *Variety* put it on another occasion, Foster was seemingly "getting through those troublesome puberty days in European films."⁹ Whatever else the European idyll might have been, it did for the most part keep her out of the gossip columns.

As 1977 ended, though, the fifteen-year-old, back in Rome to dub *Il Casotto* into English, was snapped leaving a restaurant with her *Moi, Fleur Bleue* costar Sydne Rome. The one-paragraph photo caption that ran in *People* magazine explained somewhat incongruously that "as a photographer stepped up to snap Jodie, Rome [whose baggy pants are even baggier than Jodie's partly unzipped ones] moved into the viewfinder. 'Why not?' Sydne exclaimed. 'Since we're living in a climate of feminism, it's better to photograph two women together—the worst they can say is we're lesbians.'" The anonymous captioner concluded waspishly, "Time to come home, Jodie."¹⁰

"I think if I had started out as an adult actor, I never would have made it," Jodie said years later to an interviewer who wanted to know about her child-star "horror stories." "I couldn't imagine myself going to cattle calls, having to deal with the casting couch, producers pinching me in unimaginable places. I'm glad I started out so young. It spared me all that. Can you imagine me on a casting couch? Get me out of there!"¹¹

In the new year, with *Candleshoe* about to be released in the United States, Jodie Foster was back in Los Angeles, the publicity machine again presenting her as the Disney dream teen: the brainy beauty next door. After all, despite the kitschy details that may or may not have been real, and regardless of with whom, if anyone, she might have been having sex, that was who she essentially was:

"She never does formal exercises—sit-ups, stretches and such ('They're too boring')," a teen mag reported breathlessly. "Instead, she works out by doing things she enjoys. Like walking. Swimming at a Pacific beach. And playing racquetball at least twice a week. And when she finds herself with that rare piece of free time, she might backpack it and head for the Hollywood hills to go hiking. That's when she's in California. When she's in Paris, she likes putting around on her friend's mobilette."[12]

Right.

As the 1970s tottered off on platform shoes, not to be seen again until our own time, Jodie Foster was entering young adulthood, both on and off the screen.

At the start of the eighties she had two movies to promote, *Foxes* and *Carny*, both of which showcased her acting talents in "serious" roles and reminded her peers and the moviegoing public at large that she had been nominated for a major Academy Award at the age of thirteen and ever since had been perfecting her craft and extending her range, that she was someone to whom acting mattered.

The publicity of that period, though, while paying homage to her acting gifts, almost always focused as much on Jodie Foster the gifted student about to enter college as it did on Jodie Foster the gifted actress about to enter womanhood.

She *was* a gifted student, routinely earning straight As. Foster was the French-language valedictorian of her tiny 30-student graduating class at the posh Le Lycée Français de Los Angeles (her friend from childhood on, Elizabeth Segal, daughter of actor George, delivered the English-language valedictory), in which she called herself the "little girl in blue who stands before you with tears in her eyes."[13]

Schools accepting her for that fall included Columbia, Berkeley, Stanford, Harvard, Barnard, Princeton, and Yale, among others.

Her acting career would be put on hiatus, she said, would become something to do on summer vacations—unless of course there was a great part, and then she might consider taking a semester off.

She planned to sign up for a lot of writing courses in college, and, she reiterated, eventually she planned to direct her own films; it was something she'd been saying since she was at least fourteen.

Her SAT, or Scholastic Aptitude Test, scores that year were duly reported: "robust" six hundreds, with a "stratospheric 795 out of a possible 800" in the French test.[14] So was her tour of eastern colleges, after which the well-traveled California girl concluded that "Yale is perfect. . . . The students live in rooms with private entrances, around courtyards. They have coed dorms, but I don't know if I'm ready for that. Still, I'm not crazy about living with a bunch of girls either."[15]

When she finally picked Yale, her long-absent father's alma mater, *People* magazine celebrated with a cover story that called opting for higher education the "most startling movie career decision since Garbo chose exile."[16] (Ever since, when a young woman who's achieved a measure of show business celebrity and publicly evinces an aptitude for or interest in some higher education—Brooke Shields, perhaps, or Winona Ryder—the publicity attending that declaration invariably notes that she's going to "do a Jodie Foster.")

It was a decision of which her *Foxes* Valley girl character would have approved and her *Carny* waitress character might have envied.

Her Donna in *Carny* is a sexy, sloe-eyed, small-town teenage waitress who runs away with a colorfully seedy traveling carnival, hardly the Cirque du Soleil. There she learns the ways of the circus people—the carnies and the sharpies—and the sideshow freaks: the monkey lady and the alligator man, the tallest man in the world and the fire-eating midget, the contortionist and six-hundred-pound Jelly Belly Harold, who plays guitar and has an incongruously sweet rockabilly voice.

Eighteen-year-old Donna comes between two old friends, Frankie (Gary Busey), a clown-faced "bozo" who taunts "rubes" into paying to pitch baseballs at him ("Make Bozo Splash," reads the sign above his water-filled cage), and Patch (Robbie Robertson), the carnival's all-around fixer.

"I try to ruin their relationship," Foster told one interviewer.[17]

Her character first is picked up by Frankie, then later sleeps with Patch.

Donna is the teen angel as heartbreaker. When Frankie, hurling his insults at the curious rubes from his bozo cage, first spots her on the midway, he brays, accurately, "Lookit the babyface on the teen queen!"

Significant looks and line readings give the movie an interesting subtext. When Donna expresses remorse about "getting between" the two old friends, another character, lambent-eyed Gerta (Meg Foster), who runs the string-game joint ("Step right up! Pull the string and win a prize!"), tells her, "There ain't no room in the middle of those guys," and at the end of the story there's a suggestion—never more than implicit—that Donna and Gerta may have taken up together.

This atmospheric tale, which owes an obvious debt to Tod Browning's influential circus-sideshow horror picture *Freaks*, was produced and cowritten by Robbie Robertson, best known as a musician in the Band. He also wrote the movie's effective honky-tonk midway music, and his performance as the detached and manipulative Patch is quite credible and compelling.

Set in the small-town world of diners and truck stops and traveling tent shows, *Carny* is partly about Donna's coming of age as she becomes part of the romanticized circus world. Her pivotal moment comes when she's given a chance as a barker in the string-game joint and she entices two young lesbians into spending their money.

"Pull a string, tug on it real hard," she baits one of the women, a blond who resembles her. "I know you're gonna be lucky. . . .

"Pull the string, take me home," she inveigles seductively. "I *know* you're lucky."

As the first woman strokes Donna's arm before putting up her money and taking hold of the string, her friend steps up. "We'll be in the parking lot," she says meaningfully.

The next scene is in Frankie and Patch's trailer, where, before making love to her, Patch takes the excited Donna ("I did it!" she exults. "I hustled these two chicks!") in his arms and tells her: "You don't feel like a mark anymore." Donna, by understanding the two women and exploiting their desire, has left the world of rubes and become part of the carny family.

To another interviewer Foster complained that she spent most of the time on the film's location shoot in Georgia "playing tennis. I didn't have much dialogue, so I spent much of my time improvising in front of the camera," adding, "I prefer it when the lines are given to me, when the responsibility is on somebody else. . . . The one thing about Donna is that it's the first time I'm playing a part in which age is not a factor."[18]

Age was very much a factor—in fact it was one of the central themes—in *Foxes*, which was directed by Adrian Lyne for Casablanca FilmWorks. Lyne, another of the wave of expatriate British commercial directors then beginning to make feature films in America, went on to direct *9½ Weeks*, *Flashdance*, *Fatal Attraction*, and *Indecent Proposal*, among others.

Foxes, originally titled *Ladies of the Valley*, told the story of four San Fernando Valley teenage girls growing up with absentee or abusive or infantilized parents in a Los Angeles awash in sex, drugs, and rock and roll. Lyne, deploying neon-bright colors, filtered light, and smoke machines, made it all look like a music video.

As usual, in most of the publicity Foster went to some length to distance herself from her character, Jeanie, although she admitted to one interviewer that "I had a lot of input into the character . . . and I've never worked so hard in all my life."[19] And the character she helped create, a teen growing up fast with adult-sized responsibilities and adult-sized temptations in fast-lane L.A., resembled her in more than just physical aspect.

LIKE FOSTER, Jeanie is saved from her own Kewpie-doll cuteness, and a blond Barbie-doll blandness, by wary intelligence mixed with her precocious world-weariness. Nothing will surprise this girl, who was raised in proximity to celebrity, except perhaps the imminent failure of her friends, three other sixteen-year-old girls, to overcome the uncaring world's many traps and temptations and to live up to their own better instincts.

Jeanie confides to one of her girlfriends that she "slept with a coupla guys in ninth grade, when it was new," adding: "I'm no Suzy Slut, know what I mean?"

Jeanie, like Jodie of that time, has longish straight honey-blond hair, parted neatly on one side; wears sensible, not seductive, clothes, such as white jeans with a tucked-in Hawaiian silk shirt or khakis with a vest worn over a blousy white shirt; has a hip little bop in her walk; and smokes.

In the film's best scenes, between Jeanie and her mother, Mary (played by Sally Kellerman), it is the girl who seems to be raising the insecure divorced adult woman. Coming upon her mother in bed, surrounded by open books, Jeanie asks her what's wrong. "How come you're not asleep?"

"Because I have a test tomorrow," replies the teary, forty-year-old divorcée, a touch of hysteria and reproach in her voice, "and I study for my tests."

"You're also dating a man who doesn't take you out to dinner and stands you up for his ex-wife," Jeanie shoots back, but then she crawls into the bed to read Plato to her mother, who is disconsolately curled up under the covers.

Later, during a bitter argument between the two, Mary lashes out at Jeanie's entire generation: "Are there any nice people left in the world?" she wails. "You're [all] short forty-year-olds, and you're tough ones."

THE VALLEY GIRL phenomenon may have played as social documentary in the late seventies, but by the midnineties it was back as social satire—at least for a time in one small, nonunion theater in Hollywood, where *Phoxes*, a cross-gender rendition of the film, was staged by a troupe called Scotch for Breakfast Productions.

Lines such as Sally Kellerman's plaintive cry, "Hips! You make me hate my hips," when delivered by a male actor in drag, were a "hoot" and "delirious," according to a bemused reviewer, who opined that *Phoxes* "is to traditional theater what Yellow Zonkers are to caviar."[20] Such are the avid munchings of pop culture.

FLASHBACK

The Picture on Page One

EVERYTHING SEEMED to be going so well. She was eighteen, an Ivy Leaguer, and arguably the best-known and certainly the best-reviewed young actress of her rising generation. She'd been in front of a camera since the age of three, raised by a mother who knew the business and was immersed in the turbulent times, who had taught her youngest daughter to believe it was *she* who was special and not the glamorous job.

"I think you have to know your child and her moral capacity," said Brandy Foster a few months before packing her movie-star daughter off to Yale. "There's an old Italian saying, 'You will die the way you were born.' . . .

"From the beginning, Jodie was always made to recognize her self-worth. She was encouraged to voice her own opinions on any subject. . . ."[1]

On the subject of college life, in a short first-person essay writ-

ten the summer before she went off to New Haven, Jodie fairly
shouted out her sky-high expectation and ebullient affirmation:

"Well, you may not be able to rrreally rrrelate to this, pal, but
I'm trading in my lifeguard shades for a taste of that good ol' New
Haven grime. See, here's the scoop: college depression is in the
cards for me! Yale actually invited me—little smog-ridden me—
to sink my blond teeth into its dusty brick and ivy. Just coat me
up with some eastern tsuris, grease up my hair for luck, and
watch me dive into the depths of academia. . . .

"Here I come for knowledge. . . . I mean, what a thrill it'll be
to wake up to smokers' coughs, ink-stained teeth, and faces
creased by last night's pizza. . . .

"I'll show you what it's like to be five foot three and wear
browns and grays. . . .

"New Haven, here I come!"[2]

Really living real life in the real world had become mother and
daughter's oft-stated mission. Now came the test. Jodie Foster was
living the dorm life, just one of four freshmen sharing a suite,
ensconced in neo-Gothic nineteenth-century Welch Hall at Calhoun College on Yale University's Old Campus, on her own for
the first time and on hiatus from the business. And it seemed to
be working.

If the world at large couldn't quite get over being dazzled by
this storybook turn—A Hollywood Princess in the Ivy League—
at least the students were way too cool to treat her as anything
more than just another struggling member of the incoming 1,250-
student class of 1984.

Of course, there were the annoying letters professing love and
the embarrassing, tongue-tied phone calls from some superfan kid,
who blurted out to practically anyone within earshot that he'd seen
Taxi Driver fifteen times.

But *c'est la vie*; she had advanced French, freshman English,
modern architecture, and diplomatic history to worry about;
besides, being dogged by some moonstruck boy was something
any pretty eighteen-year-old coed could expect, famous or not.

And after all, back in Hollywood, the minions of the tireless publicity machine let it be known that Jodie Foster, professional actress, was still receiving some three thousand letters a month.

Having registered at Yale as Alicia Christian Foster, her given name, Jodie got on with it, trading in her starlet silks and satins for preppie tweeds. She tried to row crew but was too small.[3] She gained weight binging on junk food, smoked too much, and hung out, showing nary a trace of Hollywood attitude.

Having spent her life until then in an adult world, she was finally spending time with friends her own age, too, including Jon Hutman, a boy from Los Angeles who went on to have his own career in Hollywood as an art director and production designer on several of Foster's films, including *Siesta*, *Little Man Tate*, and *Nell*, as well as *Heathers*, *A River Runs Through It*, and *Quiz Show*, among others.

(In latter-day Foster profiles, in fact, Hutman often has been brought in as the guest expert, as it were, with the longest perspective on both Jodie the Human Being and Jodie the Show Business Professional. In one of the best of the *Nell*-themed profiles, for example, written by Hilary de Vries, he vouched for the well-known fact that "Jodie has never lacked for confidence . . . but she has spent her career trying to stay grounded."[4] Her college life certainly began as one of the most successful of those attempts.)

"I love Yale totally," she said in the second semester of her freshman year. "I can go any place I want with my friends."[5]

After winter break, she even auditioned for and won a part in an off-campus student play, a prison drama titled *Getting Out*, in which, after a lifetime in films and on TV, she would make her stage debut as the second lead, playing, ironically, a prostitute who murders a taxi driver. Though she was back in the spotlight, this time it was student-sized and she was concerned not to upstage her peers, telling a reporter who showed up for opening night: "You have to talk about the whole play and not just me. . . . Otherwise [the other actors] will kill me."[6]

Even her mother, like any aspiring college thespian's proud parent, was jetting in from the coast to see her daughter do live theater for the first time.

The play's short run at New Haven's Educational Center for the Arts was split: two nights in late March, then performances scheduled for April 2–5, 1981. But like the Oscars that year, the show seemed like it might not go on.

A FEW SCANT HOURS before they were scheduled to air worldwide on live television, the Academy Awards were abruptly postponed for twenty-four hours. On March 31 it would be Robert De Niro who would win the Best Actor award for his portrayal of prizefighter Jake LaMotta in Martin Scorsese's *Raging Bull.*

Asked backstage the next night about the film *Taxi Driver* and its possible connection to the attack that had prompted the unprecedented delay of Hollywood's biggest night, he dodged like a boxer back-pedaling, bobbing, and weaving around the ring:

"Well . . . it's a different thing. . . . That's a loaded question first of all. I don't want to be asked that. I can't express it now. It's a terrible thing . . . but the connection . . . I have no idea. . . . It's an assumption. . . . I don't know. . . . I thank you. I said what I had to say when I accepted the award and you all look very nice. Thank you. . . ." And with that, Robert De Niro left the chaotic backstage press room.[7]

On Monday, March 30, 1981, a few minutes before 2:30 P.M., a twenty-five-year-old drifter from the wealthy community of Evergreen, Colorado, a child of privilege sunk in a mental morass of depression, fantasy, and obsession, attempted to assassinate the president of the United States as he left the Washington Hilton after delivering a speech.

Flashback | *57*

A small crowd of spectators had gathered outside for a glimpse of their new chief executive, who greeted them with a jaunty wave. From the anonymity of that admiring, cheering crowd, John Warnock Hinckley, Jr., raised a six-shot, double-action Saturday night special and fired a popping burst of .22-caliber Devastator bullets into Ronald Reagan, his press secretary James S. Brady, Secret Service agent Timothy McCarthy, and District of Columbia policeman Thomas Delahanty.

The would-be assassin was quickly overpowered at the scene. While the president was rushed away to undergo emergency surgery to remove a bullet lodged in his left lung, his assailant was taken to the marine base in Quantico, Virginia, where he was held in a closely guarded six- by ten-foot cell, under suicide watch and observation by psychiatrists.

Investigators pored over his possessions—first in his Park Central Hotel room, two blocks from the White House, then in a Denver area rooming house and elsewhere.

Found were such suggestive items as itineraries for presidential trips, a photograph of Lee Harvey Oswald and news clippings about the Kennedy assassination, a copy of *The Catcher in the Rye* (which John Lennon's assassin had also been holding the previous December when he killed the singer/songwriter in New York City), and an unmailed letter.

"Dear Jodie," began the letter, neatly handwritten on lined paper and dated 12:45 P.M., March 30, 1981.[8]

> There is a definite possibility that I will be killed in my attempt to get Reagan. It is for this very reason that I am writing you this letter now.
>
> As you well know by now I love you very much. Over the past seven months I've left you dozens of poems, letters and love messages in the faint hope that you could develop an interest in me. . . .
>
> I feel very good about the fact that you at least know my name and know how I feel about you. And

by hanging around your dormitory, I've come to realize that I'm the topic of more than a little conversation, however full of ridicule it may be. At least you know that I'll always love you.

Jodie, I would abandon this idea of getting Reagan in a second if I could only win your heart and live out the rest of my life with you. . . .

I will admit to you that the reason I'm going ahead with this attempt now is because I just cannot wait any longer to impress you. I've got to do something now to make you understand, in no uncertain terms, that I am doing all this for your sake! By sacrificing my freedom and possibly my life, I hope to change your mind about me. This letter is being written only an hour before I leave for the Hilton Hotel. Jodie, I'm asking you to please look into your heart and at least give me the chance, with this historical deed, to gain your respect and love.

I love you forever.[9]

OBSESSED WITH ACTRESS: "I Killed the President," Letter to Jodie Foster Said . . .

HINCKLEY'S FANTASY ROMANCE WITH ACTRESS JODIE FOSTER . . .

"I AM SCARED"—JODIE FOSTER: Threw Suspect's 1st Letters Away . . .

All around the world on the first of April, 1981, the picture under the headlines on page one was a publicity still, the same one, and for editors, whether at the tabloids or the *Times*, it was the obvious and only choice. But to a frightened Jodie Foster it must have seemed like a cruel and cosmic April Fool's joke, this flashback to an earlier time:

It was *Iris* . . . in her skintight hot pants and big-brimmed hat, loose curls framing that mascaraed nymphet face; *Iris* leaning

insouciantly in a doorway, thin arms crossed in front of a flow-
ery open-neck blouse tied above a bare midriff; *Iris*, the twelve-
and-a-half-year-old hooker who was the taxi driver's obsession,
who had inspired him to kill.

After two days of interviews by the Secret Service and the FBI,
once again Jodie Foster met the press. Sitting in front of a fireplace in a Calhoun College lounge, "wearing a black corduroy
jacket, red blouse and tan slacks,"[10] she read a short statement to
six invited reporters and took a few questions.

She had received "several pieces of unsolicited correspondence"
from John Hinckley in the fall and winter of 1980, she declared
in her statement. "In none of these letters and notes I received
was any mention, reference or implication ever made as to violent acts against anyone, nor was the president ever mentioned."[11]

Her aplomb was being tested publicly, and the teenager rose to
the occasion with an almost palpable formality. After all, this time
it was news—hard news—and not merely publicity.

Even while describing her horror at learning of her connection
to the man who had attempted to assassinate the president, her
low-key reserve was evident. "I must admit I was pretty jumpy.
. . . It's quite a traumatic thing.

"I acted very badly, cried I guess," she told the reporters lev-
elly. "I know it's not myself that's involved. . . . I'm in no way
involved in any of this, really."[12]

(In her own account of those events, meant to stand as her
definitive statement and published in *Esquire* magazine at the end
of 1982, Foster described a much more overwrought and hysterical reaction—laughing, crying, then laughing uncontrollably—
when she learned that the would-be presidential assassin was the
pathetically love-struck boy who'd been harassing her.)

Like her costar, she didn't want to talk about *Taxi Driver*. "I
really am not here to answer questions about [the film and the
violence it contained]," she replied to one reporter's question from
behind her arm's-length barrier of cool and careful composure.

"All I know is that it's one of the finest films I have ever seen.

It's an important film. . . . As far as I was concerned, there was no message from [it]. It was a piece of fiction. It's very relevant, but it's a piece of art. It's not meant to inspire people to do anything. It is a portrayal."[13]

While her mother looked on, Foster emphasized that she had "never met, spoken to, or in any way associated with one John W. Hinckley." That would turn out not to be the case.

Long before press agents, ad execs, and other paid media manipulators evolved into *spin doctors*, and before the word *spin* gained its current political meaning, Hollywood publicity machines were perfecting its art. Thus it should come as no surprise that, in the immediate post-assassination-attempt chaos, with her career and reputation on the line, an eighteen-year-old media-wise actress, accustomed with her press-agent mother to conditioning the spin, might have tried to limit her exposure to the media frenzy by limiting public knowledge of her contact with the accused assassin. How could she know that he'd taped the calls?

Within days after the assassination attempt, though, a wire service reported that federal officials were in possession of a tape recording of John Hinckley talking by telephone to a woman "believed to be actress Jodie Foster."[14]

Months later, when unnamed law enforcement officials confirmed that Hinckley had phoned her dorm room at least five times and taped two conversations, both in October 1980, she would say only, "It's not anything I can talk about."[15]

Transcripts of the calls, however, excerpted in a newspaper article, clearly show a young woman irritated by an unwelcome intrusion:

"As her roommates laughed in the background, Miss Foster remarked, 'Yeah, I should tell him I am sitting here with a knife.'

" 'Well, I'm not dangerous,' Mr. Hinckley assured her later in the conversation. 'I can promise you that.' . . .

"The transcripts show that Mr. Hinckley repeatedly said he just wanted to talk with Miss Foster in a midnight phone call to her dormitory room at Yale. One conversation goes as follows:

"Miss Foster: 'Seriously, this isn't fair. Do me a favor and don't call back. All right?'

"Mr. Hinckley: 'How about just tomorrow?'

"Miss Foster: 'Oh, God. Oh, seriously, this is really starting to bother me. Do you mind if I hang up?'

"Mr. Hinckley: 'Jodie, please.'"[16]

The word *fan* is derived from the word *fanatic*, which comes from the Latin *fanaticus*, meaning "inspired by the deity to a frenzy."

In addition to his taped phone conversations with Foster, the prosecution at his two-month-long trial that began in May 1982 introduced a third audiotape[17] in which the would-be singer substituted Jodie's name in a well-known ballad written by John Lennon for his wife Yoko Ono:

> In the middle of the night I call your name.
> Oh, Jodie,
> Oh, Jodie,
> My love will turn you on.

John Hinckley was not the first fan to become unhinged by what he saw on stage or on the screen, and he would be far from the last. Just a few months before, another young fanatic, lost in fantasy and imagining himself a purifying avenger, had murdered his own hero, John Lennon, on a New York street.

"It was a movie-driven man who tried to murder our first movie-actor president," wrote Garry Wills,[18] one of the most incisive observers of the Reagan era in American politics.

Growing up in what was apparently a loving, well-to-do Colorado home, John Hinckley nonetheless seemed engulfed and overwhelmed by the popular culture all around him. His first infatuation was with John Lennon and the Beatles. Traveling to

Los Angeles in the bicentennial summer of 1976, he took a Hollywood apartment and spent his time in movie theaters, watching *Taxi Driver* over and over again, buying both the novelization of the film and its soundtrack.

As his attempts to be a professional songwriter, to sell his music in Los Angeles or Nashville, foundered, and after he dropped out of college at Texas Tech, where he'd been taking journalism and literature courses, John Hinckley sank further and further into madness and fantasy.

"Living in a Dallas apartment by himself, he gained a great deal of weight. Depressed, he returned to Lubbock and spent most of his time reading Nazi literature. In September 1979, he conceived the American Front, a national organization whose goal was to alert the country to minority groups threatening the rights of white Protestants. Although this association existed only in his mind, Hinckley recorded the group's activities and wrote a newsletter for members. . . .

"In 1979, Hinckley did not return home for Christmas, telling his parents that he was meeting Lynn [his girlfriend, also a fantasy creation] in New York. . . . In reality, Hinckley stayed alone in Lubbock, playing Russian roulette. . . . Increasingly, he suffered from emotional and physical problems, including stress, weakness, and a feeling of vertigo."[19]

In May 1980, John Hinckley read in *People* magazine that Jodie Foster would be enrolling at Yale for the fall semester.

"During the summer, he wrote poems about Foster and fantasized about rescuing her from Yale as [Travis] Bickle [the character played by Robert De Niro] had rescued her character [Iris] in *Taxi Driver*."[20]

He told his parents he was going to visit his girlfriend, an actress, in New York City and that he was going to enroll in a writing program at Yale. In reality, just as there was no girlfriend, there was no writing program.

Instead, Hinckley, like Travis Bickle the taxi driver, had begun to arm himself and to stalk a politician, turning up, over the next two months, in Washington, in Chicago, and in Nashville on dates that coincided with President Jimmy Carter's campaign travels.

At the Nashville airport, Hinckley was arrested for carrying concealed weapons—two .22s and a .38—but the guns were only confiscated and he was fined $62.50, driven to the airport, and released. Four days later, in Dallas, he bought two more .22s.

In late September he also traveled to New Haven, using the $3,600 his parents had given him (from proceeds of the sale of his stock in the family oil-and-gas company) to enroll in the writing program. At Yale, Hinckley spied on Foster, slipping poems and letters under her residence-hall door. Twice he spoke to her on the telephone,[21] surreptitiously taping the awkward conversations.

Intimidated by the student scene, he returned home to Colorado after spending only a week at Yale. "Mrs. Hinckley, whose husband was out of town, was upset by her son's sudden appearance. After he explained that he didn't like Yale and that his clothes were inappropriate, she decided not to let him spend the night at home."[22] Later, both parents expressed remorse for having turned their son away on this and another occasion. But the Hinckleys were devout and fundamentalist Christians, and their creed inclined them toward strictness in matters of personal responsibility. That was reinforced by the therapist they consulted, who prescribed pills and "tough love" for John. The next morning, after spending the night in a motel, John Hinckley returned to Texas. Over the next few weeks, he traveled to Washington and Ohio, his wanderings intersecting again and again with the 1980 presidential campaign, then in its final frenzied stretch.

In early October, John Hinckley was stalking Jimmy Carter at an Ohio campaign stop, where a news cameraman photographed him only a few feet away from the president of the United States.[23] Already he was acting from deep within the deluded conviction that this was the way to win the young actress's heart—like Travis Bickle, he would kill for her.

In November 1980, the FBI alerted Jodie Foster after receiving an anonymous letter, postmarked Denver, alerting them to a plot to kidnap her from Yale. The kidnapper had a romantic motive, the anonymous tipster warned in a letter penned to seem as if it was about another person: "This is no joke! I don't wish to get further involved."

The letter's author, though, was John Hinckley.

In February and March, Hinckley returned to New Haven. In all, he'd made ten trips to the city since Jodie Foster had enrolled at Yale the September before.

Three weeks before the assassination attempt, Yale University police searched for one "John Hinckley, Jr.," the name signed to several notes and letters, hand-delivered to Jodie Foster, that the Yale freshman herself had turned over to the dean of her college on March 9.

Among those were two notes, left in early March, that read: "Just wait. I'll rescue you very soon. Please cooperate," and "Goodbye! I love you six trillion times. Don't you like me just a little bit? (You must admit I am different.) It would make all of this worthwhile."[24]

"A check through the local police department proved negative, and the attempt to find the writer was not successful" according to a Yale spokesman, who added: "The notes were considered harmless and in themselves did not present any violation of local or Federal law. . . . It must be emphasized that the significance of the notes did not become apparent until after the assassination attempt."[25]

In any case, out of money and desperate, Hinckley had flown back to Denver on the fifth of March for a final confrontation with his concerned and well-meaning parents, who, on the advice of a psychiatrist, greeted him again with "tough love," giving him money but refusing to let him come home.

"He feels that he is on a roller coaster, and cannot escape," said a psychiatrist, William Carpenter, testifying for the defense at the trial of John W. Hinckley, Jr. "He has developed . . . multiple plans for how he might remove himself from this. The plans that are most intense on his mind involve killing himself in front of Jodie Foster, shooting Jodie Foster, then killing himself, shooting to wound her and then killing himself, killing her and then killing himself. At times, he has plans, thoughts or impulses about going to a classroom, shooting the professor, the various students, and then killing himself—the classroom that Jodie Foster would be in. He also spent some time during the trips to New York looking for a young prostitute . . . he thinks is about twelve years old— again, this character Iris that Jodie Foster played in the movie—spending time searching for her, looking for her. . . .

"Of all the impulses to be destructive to others, the most persistent is the destruction of Jodie Foster."[26]

At the end of the two-month trial, the jury found John Hinckley not guilty by reason of insanity on all counts. He was committed to a Washington mental hospital.

Immediately after the assassination attempt, police had found in Hinckley's coat pocket a red John Lennon button and in his wallet a card on which was printed the Second Amendment to the U.S. Constitution (the so-called right-to-bear-arms amendment); in his hotel room they found, in addition to a note that would have been used in an airline hijacking ("I have a bomb. . . . Act naturally and lead the way to the cabin. Stay calm!"), a picture postcard of the president and Mrs. Reagan. On the back of the card was a message to Jodie Foster:

Don't they make a darling couple? Nancy is downright sexy. One day you and I will occupy the White House and the peasants will drool with envy. Until then, please do your best to remain a virgin. You are a virgin, aren't you?[27]

As events transpired in the days following the attempted assassination, it turned out that Hinckley—whose mother was nicknamed Jodie—was not the only fanatic to threaten both the president of the United States and Jodie Foster.

When Secret Secret agents arrested a young, neatly bearded, unemployed Pennsylvania man carrying a .32-caliber Smith & Wesson in New York City's Port Authority bus terminal a week after the Reagan assassination attempt and charged him with threatening the president's life, they revealed he'd been "tracked" from New Haven, where he'd spent the weekend in room 608 of the Park Plaza hotel.

After he'd skipped out without paying his hotel bill, a maid had opened up his room, and what she'd found there prompted an immediate call to the police. "In that room . . . they found [a] letter promising to carry out the assassination of the President, three .32-caliber bullets and several magazine photographs of President Reagan with X's drawn through his face."[28]

They also found a second letter that repeated the name Jodie "over and over," followed by a scrawled "I love you."[29]

Upon arriving in New Haven just four days after Reagan was wounded in Washington, this second delusional drifter had attended two performances, on successive nights, of the play in which Foster was continuing to perform against all advice from police and campus authorities.

She thought she saw him from the stage: "There was something unnerving about his emotionless stare, something I didn't trust," she wrote in her first-person account a year and a half after the event. The next night, "the strange man I had noticed the night before was again in the same seat.

"I was too pretty to kill, he had said as he was arrested. He saw me in the play and simply couldn't."[30]

Carrying on in the play must have seemed foolish to many—and in retrospect it seemed that way even to Foster[31]—but it was very much in her tough-kid/determined-woman mode and in the often-clichéd show-must-go-on tradition.

The day before his arrest, the Pennsylvania drifter had sent a letter to her, saying he'd had a "prophetic" dream:

"I will finish what Hinckley started. . . . RR must die. . . . JWH has told me so in a prophetic dream. Sadly though, your death is also required. . . . You cannot escape."[32]

Shortly after she received that chilling letter, the New Haven police received a phone call, which they traced back to the Park Plaza, threatening that Foster's residence hall would be "blown up" if Hinckley wasn't released.

But there was no bomb—only the human time bomb caught ticking down to zero in the grim and cavernous Port Authority.

Nearly three years after Hinckley exploded on a Washington street, it still wasn't over: a disturbed young woman was arrested after carrying on a correspondence with Hinckley in which, according to an FBI affidavit, "various plans were discussed, including [the woman] traveling to New Haven, Conn., to kill Jodie Foster (a student at Yale University there), and [the woman] hijacking an airplane and demanding that Hinckley, Foster and [the former high school teacher the woman was obsessed with] be brought to the airport."[33]

Life had trumped art. The petite teenager from Hollywood who'd so craved the normality of Connecticut college life was forced into guarded seclusion off campus, missing her classes and cut off from any semblance of normal student life. "I was followed all over the place," she recalled later. "I had to go around in people's [car] trunks, take freight elevators."[34]

Even Yale president A. Bartlett Giamatti expressed sympathy, declaring that she was caught in "an ancillary horror to what happened in Washington."[35]

Nonetheless, despite the horror, despite her fears, The Kid got on with it. In mid-May, protected by security guards, Jodie Foster took her freshman final exams. Two weeks later, she reported to the Los Angeles location shoot of *O'Hara's Wife*, a made-for-television movie for which she'd signed months before the assassination attempt.

In a business where even trivia gives rise to hysteria, she showed none; if anything, she seemed relieved to be back on a set and in front of the cameras.[36] Both at Yale and in the press, her poise, her common sense, and her businesslike attitude were widely admired.

"If it's a pose," one reporter observed, "she's got it down pat."[37]

"She's cool as a cucumber," the student producer of *Getting Out* said admiringly in the immediate aftermath of the assassination attempt.[38]

Said Foster herself, less than two months later, "There are a lot of things that happen in my life that . . . should scare me, but it doesn't."[39]

Surrounded by the security of cameras and cables and the bustling TV movie crew, the guarded eighteen-year-old offered a rare moment of public self-reflection:

"There are certain things that the camera picks up. People who are really crazy, you can see it. People who are really dumb, you can see that, too. It just shows on film.

"If there's one motif that I think you can pick up in everything I do, it's that I'm never wishy-washy. I may be a dumb blonde, but I'm a strong dumb blonde. It's part of what I want to portray, that strength."

A CONTINUING EDUCATION

JODIE CONTINUED TO work, to study, and, whenever possible, to avoid the press, which, in its own obsessive and derivative way, continued to adore her nonetheless, finding irresistible the strength of character and resiliency she'd summoned during and after the assassination crisis.

She'd survived, and for the professional disaster-mongers, that was sexy.

As ever, they generally swooned, too, over their own portrait of the pretty young Hollywood film actress cramming for finals between scenes on the set or of the worldly show business gypsy decamping the cloistered, boola-boola Yale life yet again for another international film shoot.

Nothing, it seemed, could dampen the ardor of the fourth estate. Nor would Jodie Foster, master of public relations, let it.

Which is not to say that she was buddy-buddy with the newspaper and magazine writers who wrote about her or the TV reporters shoving microphones at her. Trouper that she was, knowing the importance of publicity as she did, she continued to make the requisite carefully chosen PR rounds for each of her projects. But she rarely said more than she intended, regularly ruling certain subjects off-limits, and she well knew that the heedless blow-dried on-air heads and the often envious ink-stained wretches, with their manners alternately obsequious and rude, were not her friends.

Even as far back as the midseventies, as an eleven-year-old TV series star, she fairly sneered her response to the softball question of whether she would outgrow the role of Addie Pray in "Paper Moon." "I don't grow any faster than Addie does," she had ever-so-sensibly replied."[1]

In her first-person account of the events surrounding the assassination attempt[2] (many years later, she was still referring inquiring minds to the *Esquire* article, titled "Why Me?"), she says it was the "descent of the media"—not the crazed loner with the gun—that scared her the most:

"For the press my presence was almost superfluous; it was the story that counted—the twisted, bizarre headliner. A compromising photo, a brief comment was all they needed. I can't say that I didn't feel exploited by these friendly men and women with Nikons and with mikes clipped to their lapels. Suddenly they were allowed to destroy my established life because it was their job."

In a voice that sounds bitterly preppy, almost Salingeresque, on the page, she described in the same account what she considered her worst moment of the entire affair.[3] Again, the looming shadow held a camera, not a gun. One night, as she was returning exhausted from the set of *Svengali*, a TV movie shooting in New York City, "with tonsillitis and a broken clavicle and in a fit of depression," she stopped in a crowded coffee shop just as another persistent foot soldier of the insatiable media made his move:

"Suddenly, a flash of light blew up four inches from my nose.

At four inches, the photographer was just trying to harass me. The next thing I knew I was running down Eleventh Street, crying and tearing at his down jacket and slugging away. I slipped on the ice, right on my clavicle, and lay in the street, sobbing. The photographer laughed and yelled, 'I got her! I got her!' . . . I cried all the way home, all the way to my hotel room, all evening and into the night."

The bloom was off the ivy, too. Foster alluded to Yale teachers who don't "want to give you a good grade just because of who you are. It's happened."[4] And in that first-person *Esquire* account Foster reserved special scorn for those of her fellow Yalies seduced by the media's insidious blandishments—particularly the producer of her college play, "who confided to the press that I had a few problems that would iron themselves out with a little help" from him, and the "ambitious senior," whom she'd never met, who gave *People* magazine a "scoop: what I was in the habit of wearing, my favorite eating places, my friends, my classes, my dating habits—the works."

To promote one of her pictures in that period, Foster took on a new role, portraying the inquiring interviewer for a film magazine. Predictably, the questions most illuminated the questioner. "Aren't you scared by the way people tend to fall in love with you—the way they become obsessed by you?" she asked Nastassja Kinski, her *Hotel New Hampshire* costar, in the brief published colloquy. "Sometimes I wonder how much of it is really you and how much is this . . . this . . . thing you portray on screen."

When Kinski replied, with an almost audible shrug, that "things develop in [men's] heads that I can't control," Foster responded from experience: "That must scare you because you can't afford to become friends with someone without risking their obsession with you."[5] Of course, that was true of the press, too.

The fixation with the Jodie-and-John story continued to burn on, fanned by Hinckley's repeated posttrial contacts with the media, in which he aggrandizingly likened himself to the great lovers of world history. In newsrooms, bars, and wherever else wags gathered in the early eighties to exchange cynical barbs, the pointed answers to the joking questions—"Why did Mehmet Ali Agca shoot the pope?" and "Why did Israel invade Lebanon?"— were always the same: "To impress Jodie Foster."

Foster tried to stamp out the most egregious excesses, such as the publication of seminude photos of her or the network broadcast of her videotaped trial testimony, with legal maneuvers or threatened litigation. Sometimes it worked, as with the taped testimony, and sometimes, as with the photos that a magazine published, it didn't.

In the dog days of 1982, the *National Enquirer* newspaper published what Foster's lawyers called an "alleged threat" by the incarcerated would-be assassin to kill the object of his obsession. The "threat" was in the form of an explicitly violent poem called "Bloody Love," with lines like "I have come to shoot you down with my bloody gun."

Contending that the publication had violated a federal law providing for the prosecution of "whoever transmits in interstate commerce any communication containing any threat to kidnap any person or any threat to injure the person of another,"[6] her lawyers twice asked the U.S. Justice Department to prosecute the tabloid. Predictably, Justice declined.

If the media maelstrom, the baying, strobe-lit paparazzi, and the traitorous, spotlight-seeking "friends" were the worst of the ordeal, the return to work itself—first in the summer of 1981, then again in early 1982—to her place in front of the Panavision camera was what ultimately healed her. Said Foster in *Esquire*:

"I was getting restless. 'Just school' wasn't enough. As if by a stroke of fate, a script arrived, one I liked. A Manhattan location. Starring Peter O'Toole. A chance to sing. I was ecstatic . . . and, for the first time in two years, in love with a project. And *Svengali* proved a thoroughly fun film. It made me fall in love with acting again. It cured me of most of the insecurities; it healed my wounds."[7]

For the CBS television movie, she took the semester off. Critical reaction, though, suggested she should have stayed in school.

The picture updated the classic George du Maurier tale to make Svengali a jaded voice coach named Anton J. Bosnyak (O'Toole), a Hungarian émigré, who's given to declaiming in a vaguely Mitteleuropa accent and in an overwrought and operatic style teetering, perhaps tipsily, on the edge of camp, lines like "I am the teacher and you are the disciple," and "I have a power," and even "Art is a form of bondage! We are all slaves at her feet!"

HIS TRILBY IS Zoe Alexander (Foster) from Alliance, Nebraska, an aspiring rocker in her boyfriend Johnny's band.

Unlike in *Bugsy Malone*, this time Foster actually gets to sing several numbers. Belting out rock songs, her voice is Janis Joplin–ish; singing ballads, she has a pleasant Bette Midler quality. But she doesn't ever come close to the electricity that would make us believe her as the girl singer whose first album, *Getting Some Feeling Back into My Heart*, shoots up to number one.

When Zoe gets an offer from high-powered agent Eve Swiss (Elizabeth Ashley) that includes a shot at stardom and personal coaching by maestro Anton, but does not include her guitarist boyfriend or the rest of the Sleepless Knights, his band, Johnny retaliates by holding a rather intimate audition for Leslie, a new singer.

That replacement singer, who seems to have wandered in from Li'l Abner country, has to deliver such unintentionally hilarious dialogue to Johnny as "I jes' love your buns, dad gum it!" and "When I play wid a band ah don' feel raht unless ah make it with the guys." Under her black hair, blue headband, and the square-cut bangs down to her eyes, nearly unrecognizable is a future Oscar winner—Holly Hunter, named Best Actress for her role in *The Piano* and the star of *Home for the Holidays* (a film directed by another Oscar winner, none other than Jodie Foster).

ALTHOUGH HUNTER'S PART was so small as to be beneath the notice of reviewers, this TV movie is probably most distinguished as the showcase for the worst performance ever given by either actress.

The CBS television movie was a "dull, pointlessly updated rendition," according to a typical review. "O'Toole and Foster fail to light any sparks whatsoever. This has less to do with ability than with style, with O'Toole giving his character a 19th-century reading while Foster plays the archetypical hard-edged street kid. You don't believe them together for an instant."[8]

But the TV audience wasn't necessarily tuning in for that kind of verisimilitude.

Publicity shots for the picture had the forty-nine-year-old native Irishman and the nineteen-year-old California actress strolling the New York City streets hand in hand during downtime from the shoot, and the PR campaign suggested that they'd become "fast friends," a code for the nudge-nudge, wink-wink suggestion—eminently deniable of course—that they were more than just friends.

O'Toole, too, in colorful lines that sound as if they'd been penned by a publicist, saluted his costar, calling her a "gutsy little bird—a gorgeous snot-nose. As an acting team, we are absolutely spot-on. . . . The set [however] is covered with fuzz, and there are always doggy people after her. It's tremendously unfair that this nice, talented girl should have become the target for every nutter in the land."[9]

The trial of the chief "nutter," in the middle of that year, kept Hinckley and his dangerous obsession in the public eye. While Foster, perhaps prudently, vacationed in Europe, her videotaped testimony played in a Washington courtroom.

(Unbeknownst to her in advance, Hinckley himself was present at the videotaping of her testimony, which she gave a year to the day after the assassination attempt. According to some accounts, when Foster said in response to a question that "I don't have any relationship" with him, Hinckley threw a pencil at her. In any case, at the trial itself, when that answer was replayed on the videotape, the defendant, "appearing agitated," "stalked from the courtroom escorted by three federal marshals."[10]

Although Hinckley was locked away, the copycat death threats continued, and Foster's attempts at a "normal" college life—the hanging out at the Cross Campus Library, the philosophizing and talking dirty until five in the morning that she'd rhapsodized about in *Esquire*—were shattered.

Before returning to Yale in early 1983, she did a day of interviews in New York to promote *Svengali*. A wire service report had her "cherubic" (most likely journalistic code for "chubby") and dressed coedlike for the occasion, in sneakers, jeans, and an oversized blue blazer.[11]

Both her mother, in from the West Coast, and a network PR man were on hand, and it was a mark of her new wariness that "she refused to have her picture taken and would not allow reporters to use tape recorders," according to the wire service. She was quite clear, though, about her two loves—"Once you're there, there's nothing like being on location," she enthused, while Yale, she said, was "like a huge candy store," a place where once again she felt "safe." That she was still taking precautions in her movements around New Haven and still being guarded by security people were realities that it was perhaps best not to mention.

Seemingly, alternating filmmaking with schoolwork was an effective enough antidote to the existential terror of "perceiving death in the most mundane but distressing events."[12]

It was also the best antidote to the widely held but unspoken belief in Hollywood that anyone, even Jodie Foster, would be crushed under the burden of the assassination-attempt madness and that her career, promising as it was, would certainly be another casualty of John Hinckley's gunfire.

Foster, determined Yale lit major, who called herself the "kind of student who writes papers a week in advance and never misses a single class,"[13] continued steadily to make films, either during vacations or on a semester-long hiatus, all through her college years . . . and beyond.

In her junior year, Jodie Foster, student of modern American literature, and in particular of African-American fiction, starred in two films, each based on a well-known novel and directed by an influential director who first made his reputation as part of the fifties New Wave.

First, in early 1983, she checked in to the cast of *The Hotel New Hampshire*, where she found the atmosphere to be youthful and collegial—a tonic to a spirit under assault.

"Everyone in it was under twenty-five and even those who weren't were," she said enthusiastically.[14]

The Orion picture, which filmed in Quebec, was directed by Tony Richardson, who also did the screenplay adaptation. It was based on the picaresque novel by John Irving, author of *The World According to Garp*. The film's outstanding ensemble cast included Beau Bridges, Nastassja Kinski, Amanda Plummer, Matthew Modine, Rob Lowe, Wallace Shawn, and Wilford Brimley.

Foster, who was top billed, played Franny, spirited eldest daughter of the eccentric Berry clan, and Lowe was cast as her love-struck brother, John. Beau Bridges was the ardent hotelier, Win, the *Garp*-like Berry paterfamilias, and Kinski was cast as the Sarah Lawrence dropout in a ratty bear suit, Susie the Bear.

THE PICTURE SOUNDS many of the familiar Irving literary themes: a big eccentric family, whose most innocent member dies; strapping, athletic men in nurse drag; comic-opera terrorists who hatch a deadly plot; a plane crash; characters who are literally frightened to death; and other devastating bolts from the blue. It's all part of the fairy tale that, in an Irving novel, keeps displacing the quotidian details of otherwise middle-class life.

"So we dream on," says a character in a surreal, Felliniesque coda to the narrative, "inventing our lives."

The film also retains the novel's sweet, bemused tolerance for the vagaries of human behavior, so that a romantic lesbian interlude between Franny and Susie and an afternoon of epically passionate, comically played incest between Franny and John both become part of Franny's character development, allowing her to get past her own obsessions—and she's clearly a better person for both experiences.

By the end of the story, in another unexpected twist of fate, Franny becomes a movie star, and at a press conference she snarls back at a mean reporter's rude question: "That's a crock of shit!"

Doubtless that's a line that may have crossed Jodie's mind in real life, too, and in an inside joke the "mean reporter" was portrayed by the film's actual unit publicist—the person charged with dealing with the press during the production. (Also playing a reporter at the press conference was Jon Hutman, one of Foster's best Yale pals, who later went on to a career as a film production designer. This brief appearance is his only on-camera credit.)

"What makes you think you're so tough?" asks Susie at one point, challenging Franny after yet another bizarre jolt.

"I'm not so tough," Franny fires back, "but I'm smart."

"You're beautiful," Susie muses after a moment, "but you're a bitch."

"WITH NASTASSJA, I really felt we were family," Foster said, looking back at the *New Hampshire* shoot. "I really felt we were dangerous—all those things you hate about kids: catty, obnoxious, loud, saying mean things about people. I believe we achieved a certain reality you don't get in mythic films. The part where I end up sleeping with my brother and then say, 'That's it, good-bye, here's to the rest of our lives!' always touches me.

"When we finished the picture, we were all teary-eyed and drunk and we knew we would never be like this again. . . .

"It was absolute intimacy and trust. It wasn't a hierarchical thing, and it wasn't just the actors—it was also the boom man, the prop guy . . . I could have howled at the moon stark-naked and walked on that set like a crazy woman and known that I could trust them."[15]

But not, apparently, the screenplay writer. "I've rewritten parts of every film I've ever done," she said with some exaggeration on location in Paris some months later. "When you're on the set, there's a certain sense of what works and what doesn't that some guy just out of U.C.L.A. will never have. . . . On *Hotel New Hampshire*, Rob Lowe and Nastassja and I, actually all five of the lead actors, we sat down and rewrote it."[16] (Actually, director Richardson, and not "some guy just out of U.C.L.A.," is credited with the screenplay adaptation.)

The film's notices were mixed at best, but Foster's support for it remained strong even several years later. "I love that film and I think it's wonderful," she said in the early nineties. "No matter what flaws are in there, it has a heart that I've never seen ever again. Sometimes it makes me want to do the film over."[17]

(In 1994, in what certainly can be taken as a sign of respect for the acclaimed British director of *Look Back in Anger* and *Tom Jones*, and a sign of the affection with which she recalled the *New Hampshire* experience, Foster cochaired the New York benefit premiere of *Blue Sky*, Richardson's last, posthumously released film. The screening, held at Lincoln Center with a dinner following at Tavern on the Green in Central Park, benefited AMFAR, the American Foundation for AIDS Research.)

Later the same year, Foster returned to her beloved Paris to star in *Le Sang des Autres* (*The Blood of Others*), directed by Claude Chabrol and based on the Simone de Beauvoir novel set in Paris at the beginning of the Nazi occupation of France.

The screenplay, by novelist Brian Moore, was filmed both as a six-hour European miniseries and as a choppy three-hour film that aired on Home Box Office in the United States.

Starring with Foster, who was top billed, were Michael Ontkean, Sam Neill, and Stéphane Audran, Chabrol's ex-wife.

Foster played Helene, a Frenchwoman in love with Jean, a resistance fighter played by Ontkean. Neill was the German entrepreneur Bergman, also in love with Helene, and Audran played Gigi, a collaborating fashion designer loosely modeled on Coco Chanel.

THE DE BEAUVOIR STORY is a romantic wartime potboiler, with much resistance derring-do in occupied Paris and the French countryside, but its real theme is obsessive love in the very Gallic form of a triangle—a man loves a woman who loves another man who loves . . . the Cause of Liberty.

Helene, a level-headed, apolitical dress designer, loves Jean and will do anything for him, even smuggle a gun into a hotel commandeered by Nazi top brass. Bergman, a dapper Nazi entrepreneur faintly reminiscent of Oskar Schindler, is gaga over Helene.

Blood opens in 1938. While the Spanish Civil War rages and communists and fascists are battling each other in the streets of Paris, lovesick Helene follows Jean and slips love letters under his door.

"How come you didn't answer my letters?" she asks, after following Jean to the local dance hall.

"I didn't want to encourage you," he replies.

And later, declaring her love to Jean, Helene says passionately: "I'd do anything for you! I'd lie, I'd cheat, I'd steal. I'd betray my country. I'd kill someone."

When the Nazi occupiers sweep into Paris, with them comes the well-connected, tightly wrapped Bergman, who takes one look at the plucky blond Helene and loses control, offering to make her the star of the Berlin fashion world, the Leni Riefenstahl of haute couture. But unlike the real-life Riefenstahl, the talented German actress and director who became Hitler's favorite filmmaker, the fictional heroine Helene does not succumb.

"What I feel for you is a sickness," moans Bergman, filled with lust and self-disgust. "The fact that I love you may destroy me."

FOSTER, WHO HAD gained as much as twenty pounds living the student life, looks round-faced and apple-cheeked, thick and bourgeois, in some scenes; sleek and cosmopolitan in her Karl Lagerfeld–designed clothes in others—actually, just the kind of Rubenesque woman whose "cherubic" embonpoint would melt a repressed and erstwhile cultured Nazi's veneer of rationality.

For years she'd been telling interviewers that her skill was in "making eyes" at the camera, and in this picture she proved it. In scene after scene, surrounded by an "international" cast of wildly varying talent, Foster magnetized the camera with her eyes—glancing coquettishly toward it or gazing sparkly-eyed at the other actors in her scenes even when they weren't delivering lines to her.

But ultimately, Foster's emoting as Helene seems flat, without the usual textures and shading. She sounds too all-American, straight out of California, and misplaced in Paris, just as a decade later, in *Robin Hood*, Kevin Costner seemed to have wandered right off the beach and into Sherwood Forest.

It turned out that *Blood's* producers had directed their young actress not to use a French accent for the American cable version.

Foster, fluent in French, was "not happy" about the prohibition, saying caustically (and publicly) after the shoot was completed that "World War II didn't happen in Ohio. I think (the producers) are underestimating the audience, but it's out of my control."[18]

And control is *the* issue, as anyone really in show business will attest.

Although Jodie Foster had been saying since the age of fourteen that she wanted to direct, that desire now seemed more urgent, and its expression was more pointed. "As an actress," she concluded from her experience, "I only have a certain amount of power."

While the film was shooting, though, the famed director, who according to many cineastes actually began the nouvelle vague, had remarked that Foster needed no direction from him at all, because she was like her character, "very strong, very impulsive."

To which she replied, echoing her I-don't-grow-any-faster-than-the-character line of a decade earlier: "Either I am like Helene or I have made Helene like me."[19]

Image control inevitably leads to lapses, even if slight: While doing publicity rounds for *The Hotel New Hampshire* she presented herself, with more than a little justification, as the kind of serious college student who loves the rigorous intellectual life and "never took architecture or art or things like that."[20] However, three years before, in May 1981, *Interview* magazine ran her first-person interview with her own "very famous Modern Architecture professor," Vincent Scully, over whom she admitted a "slight school girl crush."

"Because books are my passion," Jodie Foster told a fashion magazine in mid-1984, "I have a really split personality: half artistic, half incredibly academic. . . . What I enjoy most is sitting down and writing a paper."[21]

A month later, she was in New Zealand, where she and her costar, John Lithgow, filmed *Mesmerized* (also known as *My Letter to George* and *Shocked*), another variation of the durable Svengali myth, set this time in the late 1800s and filmed on location.

By the time of *Mesmerized*, all trace of the chipmunk heaviness evident in *Le Sang*, the pudginess that some journalists had taken to calling her "baby fat," was gone. Costumed in long, bustled, period dresses with high, antique-lace necks, with shawls or beaded vests over her shoulders, she nonetheless looked sleek and strong, and her features were fine and delicate once again.

Again Foster was top billed, playing Victoria, a pensive, eighteen-year-old china-doll orphan married off to Oliver Thompson (Lithgow), a bearded, alarmingly beet-faced merchant, who towers over her and whom she loathes and tries to flee.

VICTORIA IS TAKEN from her beloved St. Paul's Foundling Home and school, where, between classes, the little girls splash happily in huge steaming wooden tubs, to the cosseted married life on lush and exotic North Island, a *Piano*-like locale of sylvan natural beauties and blue-tinged cloudy skies.

Wind hisses through the trees, and ominous music plays as a carriage takes Victoria to her new husband's home, where a dour servant accounts for the dimly lighted rooms by intoning that the "master likes to save a penny."

The master also likes to watch through a peephole while his new young bride undresses. With his twitchy impulses barely held in check by his straitlaced sense of propriety, one basset eye fixed firmly at his spy hole, hard-breathing merchant Oliver Thompson is an early example of what was to become a gallery of over-the-top Lithgow villains.

The film is told in flashback, with Foster, employing a charmingly soft-spoken and lightly lilting Aussie/New Zealand accent, narrating in voice-over, while her character sits in the dock of a packed courtroom, on trial for the chloroform-poisoning murder of her husband.

When the jury can't figure out how she did it (it was mesmerism, natch: she put the loathsome Oliver into a trance by waving his own shiny nosehair-clipping scissors in front of his boggled eyes and, while he was mesmerized, bade him drink the fatal chloroform), Victoria goes free, sailing away with vile Oliver's sensitive younger brother George, her lover, while the soundtrack swells with the dramatic aural theatrics of a mezzo-soprano aria from *Cosi Fan Tutte*.

THIS GOTHIC bodice ripper with mildly feminist overtones was derived, we are informed in the credits, from a "real character, crime and trial." The screenplay itself, by the film's American director, also was based on the "original work" of Jerzy

Skolimowski, the film director best known for the movies *Moon-lighting* and *The Shout*.

The film was distributed by RKO. While interesting as another example of Foster playing a Trilby figure (and therefore as grist for the pop psychologists who've found a suspicious plethora of fictional father figures in roles throughout her career), it probably is just as fascinating, at least for cinema academicians, as a comparative study of organized labor in conflict with management/producers in a distant dominion of the British Commonwealth.

Certainly at the time, it would've been of more than passing academic interest to the twenty-one-year-old Foster herself, who, in addition to top billing, had the "coproduced by" title, although it was buried in the film's end credits.

(The Hollywood trade papers, for example, seemed unaware that the picture's young star was also one of its producers, and none of the publicity, admittedly sparse, for the picture mentioned the fact.)

No sooner were Foster, Lithgow, and three other non–New Zealanders signed for *Mesmerized*, written and directed by Michael Laughlin, the American whose credits included producing *Two-Lane Blacktop*, than New Zealand Actors Equity threatened to dis-rupt the shoot, claiming the producers were violating a labor accord under which films made in New Zealand wouldn't employ more than two "imported" actors.

The picture, said an Equity spokesman, was setting a trend in which local actors would be reduced to mere "wallpaper" sup-porting the foreign talent.

"We cannot guarantee there will be silence around the Keri-keri [Bay of Islands] location or that people not in period costume will not cross the path of cameras," the spokesman threatened as the six-week shoot got under way.[22]

The producers collectively replied that, in effect, without the Yanks there would be no work at all, because without them they wouldn't have been able to raise financing; and after all, the

$2,600,000 shoot was pumping money into the local economy as well as directly providing income for 34 local actors, 445 local extras, and 75 local members of the crew.

The producers' money argument had its usual impact, and the protests didn't materialize. The picture was completed essentially on budget and on time.[23]

The accents may have been different, but the arguments, both pro and con, are to this day familiar ones in Hollywood executive suites, where "local content," trade barriers, and runaway production are still of bottom-line importance.

Years later, her production participation on *Mesmerized* long forgotten, Foster uncharacteristically shifted the blame for the picture's failure to RKO. "It was very badly produced," she declared, "and RKO said, 'Well, maybe you'll have a chance of distributing it if you make it a thriller and you take out the mesmerism.' They should have just left the edit alone."[24]

In May 1985 Jodie Foster received her undergraduate degree in literature from Yale University. Unlike the rest of her original nonfilmmaking classmates, who might be forgiven the idea that being a Yalie was by itself a full-time job, and who'd graduated in the usual public cap-and-gown ceremony a year before, she received her degree in private. There were, of course, security concerns.

By then there was no more talk of graduate school or of being an ambassador to a French-speaking country or of perhaps teaching. Foster was going to act, and she was going to direct and possibly write, she said firmly and repeatedly.

As she had for years, she continued to show respect for the *business* of show business, especially for its behind-the-scenes professionals, just as she continued to disparage the academic approach to acting, especially the Method.

(Years later she emphasized the story-driven nature of her acting and characterized the essence of acting with a single apt, but rarely used, word—"performative"[25]—very much a bright English major's word—which *Webster's Tenth* defines as "an expression that serves to effect a transaction or that constitutes the performance of the specified act by virtue of its utterance." Examples of performatives are the phrases "I bet" or "I declare war."

Around the same time, she summarized her own naturalistic method as an acting instruction to Adam Hann-Byrd, a seven-year-old novice actor playing the title role in *Little Man Tate*: "Just pretend really well, and then think about what that pretending looks like."[26])

Jodie Foster left Yale as she had entered it: without once having set foot in an acting class.

During her college years, in addition to the usual Ivy League academic grind, she had published articles in two national magazines and had made five films—three for television (*O'Hara's Wife*, *Svengali*, and *Le Sang des Autres*) and two for theatrical release (*Mesmerized* and *The Hotel New Hampshire*).

She had majored in modern American literature, switching to it from classical lit.

Her favorite authors, according to a mideighties PR biography, were Toni Morrision, eventual Nobel Prize winner and the subject of her senior thesis, and perennial lit-major favorite John Fowles, author of, among many others, *The Collector*, *The Magus*, and *The French Lieutenant's Woman*—all novels that can be interpreted as being about innocents caught up in the web of a dangerous obsession.

Where once she had turned up in backpack, T-shirt, and jeans in such magazines as *Seventeen* and had been described elsewhere as turned out in "lumberjack chic," to publicize her pictures in her immediate post-Yale years she posed for such renowned photographers as Annie Liebovitz and Helmut Newton in femme fatale photo layouts in *Vanity Fair*, *Vogue*, and *Mademoiselle*. She was, according to the same PR bio, now a resident of Los Angeles, California, and Paris, France.

"Images are usually pretty true, unless you perpetuate some stupid image of yourself," Foster said. "I think the industry probably sees me as a whiz kid, just because I speak well. If you speak well, you must be smart. Plus going to college, which everybody knew about . . . not that it taught me to be smart." Asked if people were intimidated by her, Foster replied: "Initially, yeah, which I think is very funny. People become defensive. But everybody's image precedes them."[27]

Jodie Foster thought of herself simultaneously as a loner and as a team player. She was known internationally by millions, submitted herself when business dictated it to interviews in the mass-market media, yet remained intensely private and guarded.

Recalling her high school days, she said, "Now I'm very social but then I was a loner. I don't regret it," before gratuitously offering what reads as a very revealing remark: "That's why I don't go to a woman gynecologist," she said without any prompting. "She'll know too much. With guys you can get away with a lot of stuff."[28]

Whether disinterested or nonplussed, her interviewer didn't take up the thread, immediately asking instead about her favorite childhood movies.

"Foreign films," she replied decisively. "My mother was a Francophile, although she didn't speak French. We saw a lot of foreign pictures."[29]

The intimacy/trust issues raised by the gynecology comment remained offstage.

Jodie Foster's next picture was *Siesta*, the first feature film from Mary Lambert, director of Madonna's early breakthrough music videos, including those for "Material Girl" and "Like a Virgin."

Foster—playing Nancy, an upper-class Brit sophisticate whose dissolute-artist companion, Kit, was played by Aubrey Beardsley-lookalike Julian Sands—was part of a strong cast that included Ellen Barkin, Gabriel Byrne, Martin Sheen, and Isabella Rossellini. Its music was composed and performed by none other than Miles Davis.

This fine ensemble was marooned, however, in a pretentious, overly symbolic story, based on a novel by Patrice Chaplin, that confused audiences and alienated many critics, about Claire (Barkin), a California skydiver in Spain, in love and literally (and repetitively) on the run in a red sundress.

It's the kind of movie where Claire, the bruised mystery babe who wakes up at the edge of an airport runway, isn't wearing underwear when she strips off that sundress to wash off . . . blood. *Who has she killed?* she wonders in voice-over. *Who's dead?*

The dialogue, too, set critics' teeth to gnashing—"This insane party has got to stop!" moans one anguished guest trapped in the Buñuel-ish goings-on into which Claire wanders, and another pontificates to the blond skydiver that "The only falling that doesn't mean failing is falling in love." And although years later the critics would wax rhapsodic over the same device as used in *Pulp Fiction,* they generally hated *Siesta*'s fractured narrative time frames, too.

Foster's Sloane Ranger character, her hair pulled back and tied with silk scarves, a champagne flute practically grafted to her hand, was the "idiot child of this century," she said dismissively later, "a real airhead."[30]

Foster acts her with uptilted chin and a single bony shoulder blade pushing forward for emphasis, on her face in moments of conflict or passion a look of *Isn't this so-o-o-o delicious?* Under some stress, Nancy copes by studying her face in a compact.

"Born to be beautiful, born to be dizzy" is how another character enviously describes her.

Foster's Nancy, whose single costume is a deep blue dress under a matching jacket with white trim, dials up "Mummy" whenever she needs money or an airline ticket. Meeting Claire in a lavatory, where they've both gone to escape the party from hell, she blithely announces that "here I am in a bathroom, utterly pissed, alone on my birthday, without love, without money, asking myself"—here she interjects a tiny, well-bred haw-haw—"what else is there?"

"Ambition and a half hour of primetime TV," replies Claire.

As sometimes happens in Hollywood, the picture was a misbegotten labor of love. Said director Lambert: "*Siesta* got made because a lot of people put faith in one another. . . . Nobody made any money. Everybody worked on deferments. I knew it was a house of cards. I had my life staked. It's a stressful, scary way of doing something."[31]

As usual, Foster's notices were stronger than those of the film itself, which one critic called an "extremely strong contender for the most irritating movie of the year. It mushes all the most grating qualities of the European 'art' film into one unendurable hash."[32]

To what could have been a simple walk-on and a walk-through, in a picture that aimed to be that year's *Blue Velvet* but only achieved a kind of "perfume ad surrealism," Foster brought much more, said another critic, who left off lambasting the film to praise "Jodie Foster's twittering embodiment of Noël Coward decadence. *Siesta* has scarcely more depth than a student film, but Foster larks out on an acting class exercise and erases everyone in range from the screen. The real question isn't what the fuck Claire's doing in Spain, but when is someone going to come up with a movie to match Foster's potential?"[33]

The wait for that movie, which had lasted at least since *Foxes*, was coming to an end.

Jodie Foster, the self-proclaimed control freak, had taken to talking publicly about her own inner turmoil, but only retrospectively, and she did it with a decorum rare for true-confessions Hollywood:

As a twenty-year-old, she could publish a very personal, albeit a calculated and literary, essay about her teenage trauma after the Hinckley assassination attempt.

In her twenties, she also could speak about her loneliness in high school, at Le Lycée.

As a thirty-year-old, her career newly ascendant, she could finally talk about the self-doubts that had plagued her in her twenties, leading her to contemplate leaving acting entirely: "I wouldn't have said so then, but I was very unhappy. The feeling of not knowing everything you don't know . . . it was awful. All that panic."[34]

In the post-Yale eighties, Foster repeatedly gravitated toward ensemble pictures and small, serious films. In these movies she could be part of a group while standing out from it.

Five Corners, set in 1964, with the civil rights movement and the siren call of the midsixties counterculture threatening to upset a fondly remembered Bronx neighborhood's ethnic certainties, was such a picture.

It was a dark, urban version of the *American Graffiti* coming-of-age story; an independent film, directed by sometime actor Tony Bill from a quirky John Patrick Shanley (*Moonstruck*) script, made outside the constraints of the Hollywood blockbuster mentality; if it simply made a profit, said Foster, everyone concerned could breathe a sigh of relief and go on to the next project.

In it, Foster was top billed among a solid cast that included Tim Robbins and John Turturro.

And although she was still declining to comment when asked the inevitable Hinckley question, in the film she was sounding familiar themes, once again playing a character with an absent parent (her father is only seen snoozing in the background) and a dangerous, unwanted suitor (Turturro).

She plays Linda, a polite and proper girl in a madras-plaid dress, with her blond hair in a Sandra Dee/Gidget flip, who works in her father's pet shop and is the object of a deranged neighborhood boy's romantic obsession.

Turturro's obsessed and violent character knocks Linda unconscious in the final reel and carries her off to the tenement apartment where his dotty mother lives. In the picture's single most chilling scene, while Linda lies unconscious, Turturro goes in a single beat from speaking emotionally, even tenderly, with his mother to—without any warning—hurling the old woman out the window to her death.

With the film's obvious echo of the deranged character who'd stalked Foster in real life, Turturro was acutely aware of "not wanting to cause [Jodie] any [discomfort] because it was a strange movie, not wanting to cause her any grief because of everything she'd been through."

He remembers her as "really supportive . . . even helpful in scenes where she was supposed to be laying there unconscious," particularly in the crucial defenestrating-mom scene. "The director was having problems with it. . . . [He] wanted us to be wrestling and I just wanted to do it just by talking to each other. She was very supportive of that."

"I've never done a megabudget movie. I never had a limo carting me home. Never wanted one," Foster said in a brief *Mademoiselle* profile that appeared just before *Five Corners* and *Siesta* were released.[35]

(The two pictures were in theaters within a month of each other; at the time they were two of four Foster films that hadn't yet been released. The other two were *Stealing Home*, a baseball-themed love story for which her notices were so glowing that a number of critics touted her for an Oscar nomination, and a picture then titled *Reckless Endangerment*.)

As in *Siesta*, Foster was last billed in *Stealing Home*, a slice-of-life "inspirational" picture, codirected and cowritten by Steven Kampmann and Will Aldis, that also starred Mark Harmon, Blair Brown, and Harold Ramis. Foster, though, plays the character around whom the others revolve: She's Katie Chandler, a free spirit who starts out as ten-year-old Bill Wyatt's baby-sitter and ends as the college-age Bill's lover.

The narrative unfolds in multiple flashbacks with voice-overs by the adult Billy (Harmon), a wastrel, returning home after Katie's suicide. His recollections of Katie ("Katie was so wild and she hated rules. That's why she was the perfect baby-sitter") and the course of his life eventually bring him to the realization that he's got to pull himself together and pursue his childhood dream—a career in baseball—a dream that Katie wholeheartedly ratified.

Stealing Home has its enthusiastic partisans—the late-fifties, early-sixties rock and roll soundtrack, and Foster's incarnation of a sunburned golden-blond WASP, the sixties ideal of the well-off, self-confident suburban Philadelphia girl who summers on the Jersey shore, are certainly the two biggest reasons why.

Working on the picture with two first-time codirectors (a writing team responsible for, among others, *Back to School*) was an opportunity for the "collaborative" input she so prized, Foster said at the time, and there are two Katie speeches, both often cited by the film's fans, that sound like pure Jodie.

In the first, tooling down the highway in a red Cadillac convertible with her reluctant ten-year-old charge, wearing shades and a violet head scarf, Katie explains what girls like about boys: "Girls like guys who make 'em laugh," she says. "Girls like guys who talk about somethin' other than themselves and who don't break their heart. And girls like guys who smoke. Let's smoke!" And she pulls out the cigarettes.

In the second speech, almost a decade later in the narrative's time, Katie and Billy are walking along the Jersey shore. She tells him that she's getting married and moving to Europe. With an infectious dancing enthusiasm, she describes how it's going to be: "We're going to go everywhere, we're going to do everything! We're going to go to Pamplona and run with the bulls, we're going to go to Paris and smoke lotsa hashish and go to the opera, hang out at the Left Bank, you know, talk about existentialism and revolution. Who cares! It's going to be great!"

The September 1987 profile in *Mademoiselle* had several elements in common with almost every mention of Foster in print around this time: that she had a formidable reputation as a pro and a survivor and was made of "tough stuff"; that she showed no trace of "star" behavior nor seemed to require star treatment;

and that she'd made the same number of pictures as her age—twenty-four.

"I like being with all the people on a set and working among the technicians," she said while on the *Five Corners* location. "Not very glamorous, but it's the part I like best. Long hours and wretched food! Like going to school."[36]

But then again, Jodie Foster always did like going to school, and movie sets had become her own personal classrooms.

"Making movies isn't [about] going out and pitching a fucking script. . . . It's not about getting a table or being in L.A.," she said during the publicity push that preceded *The Accused.* "I know how to go to meetings and sell myself . . . but that's not what I do. What I do happens in Podunk, Iowa, and lasts two months. And what gives me my sanity and security is that it's a blue-collar job, that it's not glamorous, that it's a bitch."[37]

But making friends with the crew was more than just common sense and smart business. It was self-protective, too. "It's like, 'I'm going to bare my breasts now and you'd better take care of me.'"[38]

Still, the star student was genuinely interested—she knew about lights and filters and camera lenses and focal lengths—and that fascination enchanted her coworkers. She even knew film crews, telling one interviewer that the "best crew is a New York crew on location outside of New York City" and adding, apropos of the *Stealing Home* company, that a "cynic in suburbia is a wonderful sight to see."[39]

Foster was known for the long hours she liked to spend on the set, time when she could have been elsewhere. Most movie stars couldn't wait to play hooky, typically rushing away from their scenes on location to their lavishly appointed Winnebago trailers, those small kingdoms where they could pass the hours of tedium until the next "call," surrounded by their own agent, their personal hair and makeup person, a gofer, and whoever else was part of their "professional family." Backslapping badinage motivated by self-interest was as good as their relationships with the blue-collar majority of their crews ever got; after all, a disgruntled lighting technician could play havoc with a carefully wrought image.

Foster liked to work, too, and she'd been doing it a long time, so when she turned thirty she could still say she'd made the same number of films as her age, as she could when she turned thirty-two. It's a boast that she'll probably still be making as an octogenarian.

"That sounds as if it were some grand plan now, doesn't it?" Foster remarked in a typical comment. "It is grand. . . . But there was no plan. I've been doing this for so many years that I'm more comfortable in front of a camera than anywhere else."[40]

It was something she'd been saying for years, as was the oft-repeated insight about learning from adversity: "You learn from hardship and disappointment. You don't learn from winning an Oscar or making a million dollars a year."[41]

The first part of that assertion she knew from experience: Despite her self-doubts, she hadn't folded under tough going. The second was about to be tested.

OSCAR AND INNUENDO

JODIE FOSTER MADE
a low-budget picture in Vancouver, Canada, that the producers had doubted she'd be right for.

It wasn't politic to say it in so many words, but like everyone else in Hollywood they still thought of her as the chubby little coed from the early eighties, not thin enough to play an anorexic in a television movie: an actress who even refused to have her picture taken and was wary of the press! Talk about the career portents being bad.

She'd made a lot of arty movies in the early and mideighties, too. *Art* may be a compliment, and to attempt it—regardless of results—still may be noble in parts of the world, but not in Hollywood, where all too often *art* is synonymous with *noncommercial*. It certainly was, in picture after picture, in Jodie Foster's case.

Even her mother, then her manager and closest adviser, and usually so savvy about her youngest daughter's career moves, suggested, on the very verge of the end of her long noncommercial streak, that "now [Jodie] has to hang in until she's thirty-five, when the great parts for women begin again."[1]

Later, in possession of a certain gold statuette, Foster could look back and safely admit of those years in the early and mideighties that "I spent a lot of time acting like I thought everyone else on screen was an idiot, and that is the total sign of someone not committing to their work."[2] And even though she said, convincingly, that she had contemplated getting out of the business and going back to graduate school, more than one critic knew that here was an actress just waiting for the right creative spark.

Still, the producers—Stanley Jaffe and Sherry Lansing, who together later went on to run Paramount Pictures—had nearly passed on Glenn Close for *Fatal Attraction*, and that, according to Lansing, had "taught us the lesson to test everyone."[3] So Jaffe met with Foster, and reluctantly the producers agreed to let her do a screen test for their next film.

What they wanted to see, said the picture's director, Jonathan Kaplan, a strong Foster booster, was "whether she was fat or not. . . . Jodie knows that was why she was going to meet [Jaffe]."[4]

Foster herself, according to all accounts, accepted with equanimity and her usual professionalism what another lifelong denizen of the town of big egos would have seen as humiliating.

"At some point, you've got to accept that you're an object," she said later. "It's not personal, but ultimately somebody's going to say your voice sucks and your body sucks, too. You have to learn to make the personal not so personal."[5] Still dubious, the producers nonetheless agreed to go ahead with the test.

Recollections of her crucial taped audition, reading her working-class character's lines for the first time, have a *Rashomon*-like quality. According to Lansing, a former model, Foster "wore a black short skirt and a black revealing top," but Foster remembered it differently, saying she would "never wear anything overly 'babe' to a reading.

"It's like putting on a postman's hat at an audition to play a postman. It's tacky. I thought they wanted to see a tough girl. So I wore a black sleeveless turtleneck, black jeans, and cowboy boots. I wasn't prepared at all for that stupid screen test. I didn't know any of the lines. [The director] threw me in a room for ten minutes and I learned a five-page-long monologue."[6]

Later, director Kaplan recalled Lansing's initial reaction, simple and eloquent, after seeing the test play out on screen. "She just said, 'The envelope, please.'"[7]

THE MOVIE, first titled *Witness*, then retitled to avoid confusion with a Harrison Ford thriller that also starred actress Kelly McGillis, was called *Reckless Endangerment* while it was shooting. Later, the movie was retitled again.

Foster was second billed as Sarah Tobias, an actual working-class girl who was gang-raped in a bar while onlookers cheered on her attackers, while McGillis had top billing as Katheryn Murphy, the assistant district attorney who prosecuted both the rapists and their instigators.

As the picture was shooting, it was engulfed by a firestorm of hot gossip, which in Hollywood can arise with Santa Anna suddenness and will turn out to be false about as often as it is true. The rumor that was sweeping the power-lunching elite: The two costars were having a torrid affair.

In Hollywood gossip is treated as gospel, and change is automatically suspect, and almost every big studio release has its shadowy detractors—often because of personality conflicts and studio politics (for example, before it was dispelled by people actually seeing it in early screenings, a bad-word-of-mouth whispering campaign preceded *E.T. The Extra-Terrestrial*, reflecting an internal battle between two warring camps, one pro Spielberg, one anti, at the studio)—but the prerelease "buzz" about the Foster-

McGillis picture itself and their performances in it remained excellent. This year's *Fatal Attraction*, the prerelease handicappers said.

THE ACCUSED, as it was finally called, was based on the true story of a lone woman gang-raped in 1983 on the pinball machine in a tavern in the working-class town of New Bedford, Massachusetts. Drunken bystanders had cheered on her attackers. In the picture the rape occurs in 1987, the bar is called The Mill, and the town itself, with its leaden skies like low expectations, is never identified.

Because Tobias herself was "merely" a waitress, had been drunk at the time, was wearing a "sexy" outfit, and drove a Camaro with the vanity license plate *SXY SADI*, while one of her attackers was a local college boy, townspeople treated her as if she'd been "asking for it," had deserved to be raped. "What the hell difference does it matter how I was dressed?" Sarah demands irately of the young assistant DA who's been questioning her. "They tore it offa me."

After assistant DA Murphy cuts a deal to put the three rapists in jail for "reckless endangerment," a felony that carries the same jail time as rape without the sex-crime connotation, Tobias is outraged and feels betrayed. "I never got to tell nobody nothin'," she says. "You did all my talkin' for me."

Despite being discouraged by her colleagues, Murphy realizes she has to take the barroom onlookers to court. Because they shouted such encouragements as "Get her! Go on! Do it! C'mon," she charges them with "criminal solicitation," for "getting the rape going and keeping it going," and Tobias testifies against them.

Foster's Sarah Tobias may have demanded justice and gotten it, but she never asks for pity. Foster played her expertly, drawing on all the tough girls she'd incarnated over the years to produce a voice that was raw, a scratched whisper pitched to a register that suggested, rather than expressed, hysteria and tears.

"I heard somebody screamin'," she says quietly, when first describing the attack, "an' it was me."

"Are you married?" asks the assistant DA as she's driving the bruised Sarah home from the hospital.

Sarah replies with a line that must have resonated with Jodie: "My ma was married ten years, but he left when I was born."

HARDEST OF ALL the scenes to film, according to Foster, was not the brutal rape scene, although it took several bruising, emotional days to shoot, and blood vessels in her eyes burst from repeated crying, but the "humiliating" moment earlier in the narrative when Sarah, alone and intoxicated, does a solitary dance to the jukebox music, oblivious to the hostile, predatory eyes watching her every swaying move.[8]

After the shoot was finished, Foster said repeatedly, all she wanted to do was hit the clubs and dance. "I don't know what comes over me," she said. "For three weeks I have to go dance. I go to all the clubs and spend three hours on the dance floor with my friend just having convulsions. . . .

"Then I go back to the Valley, where people don't want to hurt you. When I'm away from there, I always feel like everyone wants to hurt me."[9]

Regardless of whether or not they were intimate—and the hostile, predatory eyes of Hollywood were utterly convinced that they were, with detailed stories of the supposed tempestuous affair circulating widely (though one of the few persons even to allude to the gossip on the record, staunch Foster booster and *Accused* director Jonathan Kaplan, called it "so not true that it's insulting"[10])—Jodie Foster made no secret of the fact that she and her costar were close and that she regarded Kelly McGillis, a Juilliard-trained actress, professionally with something approaching awe.

"Ask her to cry and she can say, 'How much? Which eye? When?'" said Foster shortly before the film was released.[11]

She told another interviewer around the same time that

McGillis "has really taught me things. Some had to do with her training, but most came from the way she thinks and feels. I say things off the top of my head, but when Kelly says something it's usually dead-on. She really knows what she's talking about. She's completely astute, never haphazard like I tend to be. She's also deeply emotional. I'm not saying I'm not emotional, but I've had to live in a different world than Kelly has; it hasn't hardened me, but it's given me sunblock. Kelly doesn't repress anything. She's very real and she doesn't lie. She can't. She doesn't know how to."[12]

In the post-Yale years, exercise had become Foster's new enthusiasm, and she and McGillis worked out together, talking about things like the "two greatest lines that boyfriends give you."[13]

(In Foster's retelling, they were "You're an actress. How can I ever trust you?" and "You went to college and you think you know everything.")

During the shoot, while the picture was still called *Reckless Endangerment*, she, McGillis, and director Kaplan had "connect[ed] in a basic, homebody way," Foster said. "I could have a spat with Jonathan like I would with my brother, and the next day I'd apologize and it would all be forgotten. It's like family with Kelly too. Pretty soon after I met her, I felt she was my sister."[14]

Finally Foster had a role to match her gift, and the accolades and awards followed predictably.

Of all the awards handicappers in Hollywood, only one showbiz vet may have been surprised. When *The Accused* shoot was over, Jodie Foster, Yale B.A., went out and took her Graduate Record Exams. "I was gonna go to Cornell," she said five years later, "and be a grad student in literature, and no one would ever hear from me again. I'd be found out as a fraud. The film was just very provocative for me personally."[15]

How provocative? "Here's how bad it got: After I got the part, I never bothered to read the script again. I got to the set and bullshitted about the story. I was acting so cool, and now, when I think about it, I was petrified."[16]

She won the National Board of Review's nod as Best Actress

and was part of a three-way tie, along with Sigourney Weaver for *Gorillas in the Mist* and Shirley MacLaine for *Madame Sousatzka*, for a Hollywood Foreign Press Association Golden Globe as Best Actress (Drama).

Hollywood's foreign press had long loved the multilingual actress, as had their colleagues abroad, dating back as far as *Taxi Driver*. For *The Accused*, Foster once again did her own French-language looping, as well as going on a five-country, three-week personal promotional campaign for the picture in Europe.

In the late eighties it was still the rare movie star who could see that the future of the American film business was in the international marketplace, and *The Accused* didn't fit the male-dominated, action-adventure pattern of the pictures that did well overseas. So when *The Accused* bettered its North American box-office take with the revenue flowing back to Hollywood from abroad and generated public debate about rape and its victims in the traditionally macho Latin countries in southern Europe, it was Foster and her tireless efforts who, deservedly, got the credit.

Foster toiled "nine to six" in Europe, enthused a studio marketing/distribution vice president at the time, being interviewed every day for three weeks and even having "a go" at speaking Italian in a Rome press conference for approximately forty local journalists. The trip, the veep concluded, established Foster "without a doubt as an international star who has brains up top."[17]

While she was away toiling in the Italian box-office vineyards, back home in Tinseltown the motion picture academy announced its annual Oscar nominations.

The Best Actress nominees for that year's Academy Awards were Glenn Close for *Dangerous Liaisons*, Foster for *The Accused*, Melanie Griffith for *Working Girl* (for which she'd already won as Best Supporting Actress at the Golden Globes), Meryl Streep for *Ironweed*, and Sigourney Weaver for *Gorillas*. (Weaver was also nominated in the Supporting Actress category for *Working Girl*.)

Foster had learned of the nomination as she was about to board a plane in Rome, she said later, where she'd bought the dress she was going to wear to the Oscars—a short, strapless, form-fitting, aqua-colored number with a big bow in back that she'd spotted in an Italian boutique window.[18]

She came to the award show at the end of March 1989 with her *Siesta* costar, Julian Sands, her mother, and other family members.

When her name was announced, "she kissed Julian Sands, her brother, and her mother, and tugged up her blue décolletage before she walked down the aisle, giving a second tug at the top of the stairs just to make sure nothing peeked out."[19]

Unlike the grand and lengthy remarks that were customary for the major acting-award winners, Jodie's speech was among the simplest and best received of the evening. It certainly was the most eloquent.

"This is such a big deal," she said, "and my life is so simple.

"There are very few things—there's love and work and family. And this movie is so special to us because it was all three of those things. And I'd like to thank all of my families, the tribes that I come from, the wonderful crew on *The Accused*, Jonathan Kaplan, Kelly McGillis, Tom Topor, Paramount, the Academy, my schools . . . and most importantly, my mother, Brandy, who taught me that all my finger paintings were Picassos and that I didn't have to be afraid. And mostly that cruelty might be very human, and it might be very cultural, but it's not acceptable. Which is what this movie's about. Thank you so much."

Backstage in the chaotic Oscar pressroom, the newly anointed Best Actress was asked what she planned to do with the golden statuette.

"For the moment, he's going to stay in these hands. He's not going anywhere. Prisoner of Jodie," she replied, chuckling. "I rented three videos last night at the video place, and they said if I brought this in I would get them free. So you can bet this is going back to the store tomorrow."[20]

It sounded just like the simple life she'd proclaimed in her acceptance speech, but normality for Jodie Foster had always been a role fraught with dangers.

Said a disembodied voice over the PA system before she came backstage, "Please, no questions regarding Mister Hinckley. This is Oscar night."[21]

Following the Oscars, the Best Actress of 1988 returned to her most difficult recurring role: normality.

Even months later, she said, being Best Actress was hard to believe. "Pleeeease. Ridiculous. Sometimes I'm driving down the freeway, and I'll just start laughing."[22]

(The feeling has persisted. As recently as the *Nell* campaign, she was repeating the driving-down-the-freeway-and-laughing line to interviewers who wanted to know how it felt to be one of the most powerful women in Hollywood.)

"It just hits me," she added back in 1989. "It's scary too. What if I fail next? What will people say?"

What people said was "Did you see Jodie Foster is one of the Ten Most Beautiful Women, according to *Harper's Bazaar*?"

She, however, said "I'll spend $50,000 on traveling, but I won't spend $200 on clothes"[23] and adamantly remained the unaffected Valley girl who loved the outdoors and wore little makeup and could blend anonymously into a midday restaurant crowd before dropping off a pile of dirty laundry at her mom's house. "I love chores," she told yet another bedazzled interviewer. "I don't want to give that up and let someone else do it—that's not living. But it's not easy. I have a lot to do."[24]

And the best part was that it was all true, too. Everyone said so.

Said a childhood friend, who had remained close: "I think she would do anything to remain inconspicuous for the rest of her life."

But after all, remaining inconspicuous would have been easy. All the Best Actress would have had to do was stop acting; after all, Hollywood insiders, both pre- and post-Hinckley, had counted her out at almost every phase of her career: too androgynous, too overweight, too freaked out, too tarred by association. Hey, most child actors didn't even make it past puberty. Her mother, Brandy Foster, wise in the ways of show business, had been the first to tell her so.

But beyond normality there was excellence. And Jodie Foster, the little trouper grown up, had always been ready to pay the price for excellence—to hit her marks or her books, to go through her paces and pay her dues, to do what the implacable Industry expected before it would embrace you as one of its own.

She may have craved normality, but one of the most important lessons she learned at Yale, one that stood her in good stead back on gossipy Hollywood sets, was that it was OK to stand out, even though the process hardened you, gave you what she had called a year and a half before winning the Oscar, "sunblock" and "sunscreen."

"Women are weird," she began reflectively. "Men start out liking themselves; women have to learn to like themselves. It takes longer for women . . . especially in the movie industry, where you walk into a room and everybody has an opinion. . . .

"So then comes the sunscreen. Maybe that's the flaw in my character that's grown out of the industry: If someone doesn't like me, I can change. You want me to be more animated? Less this or that? I can adapt myself to what people need. . . .

"My pat line is that good actors are schizophrenic in a figurative way. . . . Everybody is, they just don't know it."[25]

One actor who'd been schizophrenic, and had the certification to prove it, was Dennis Hopper, who'd hung out with James Dean, directed *Easy Rider*, and then gone into a drug-induced tailspin that had landed him comatose in a sanitarium. The power-lunching gossipers traded delicious stoned-Hopper stories—*What a talent! What a shame!*—and just assumed he'd fried his brain to a tabula-rasa crisp. It wasn't just Hollywood that had given up on Hopper, but his doctors too; still, he'd proven them all wrong, survived, and come back.

After *The Accused*, Foster said repeatedly that she was looking for something solidly commercial, but it was in *Backtrack*, a

(Yoram Kahana, Shooting Star)

Johnnie Whitaker (best known from television's "Family Affair") and Jodie in *Tom Sawyer*, their second picture together. By then, Jodie had already acquired a reputation for looking sweet but playing feisty.

(SS, Shooting Star)

Long before she became a teenager, Jodie's most important real-life role was as her family's breadwinner.

(Yoram Kahana, Shooting Star)

Years after Jodie's controversial portrayal of the preteen prostitute in *Taxi Driver*, John Hinkley's attempted assassination of President Ronald Reagan had "Iris" on the front page of every newspaper in the country. (Motion Picture and Television Photo Archives)

From the movie *Bugsy Malone*. Years later the director said that if he'd known she was going to be a big star, he wouldn't have dubbed Jodie Foster's singing voice. (Academy of Motion Picture Arts and Sciences)

The young ladies of the Valley: Cherie Currie, Marilyn Kagan, Jodie Foster, and Kandice Stroh in *Foxes*. (Len Hekel, Shooting Star)

Jodie and Sally Kellerman, daughter and mother in *Foxes*.

(Len Hekel, Shooting Star)

Jodie as Donna, dolled up for the midway strip show in *Carny*.

(Academy of Motion Picture Arts and Sciences)

Jodie's performance in the 1988 film *The Accused* established her as one of the major stars of the decade. Ironically, just before the picture catapulted her onto the A-list, she had considered leaving the business entirely. (SS, Shooting Star)

In 1989, Jodie won her first Best Actress Academy Award for her performance as Sarah Tobias, the survivor of a brutal rape, in *The Accused*. (Eddie Garcia, Shooting Star)

Jodie, as Clarice Starling, bootstraps her way through FBI training in the Academy Award–winning film *The Silence of the Lambs*.
(Orion, Shooting Star)

She always really wanted to direct, and her Academy Award gave her the clout to do it: Jodie behind the lens with young Adam Hann-Byrd, who played the title role in *Little Man Tate*. It was Jodie's first time at the helm of a motion picture. (Suzanne Hanover, Motion Picture and Television Photo Archives)

On-screen chemistry: Jodie and Richard Gere in a scene from the poignant Civil War drama *Sommersby*. (Motion Picture and Television Photo Archives)

Jodie finally appeared in a summer blockbuster, demonstrating her skill at light comedy in *Maverick*. (Andrew Cooper, Motion Picture and Television Photo Archives)

A smile, a sense of humor, and her quick intelligence make Jodie a favorite of the Hollywood press and paparazzi.

(Ron Davis, Shooting Star)

Jodie and Randy Stone
at the 1995 Academy
Awards.

(Ron Davis, Shooting Star)

Jodie, a self-described
homebody, usually
comes out for
Hollywood events only
as part of a publicity
campaign for her pic-
tures or during the
awards season, but she
looked at ease at the
premiere of *The
Shawshank Redemption*.

(Ron Davis, Shooting Star
International)

film directed by and costarring Hopper, lately resurrected as the great sixties survivor, that Foster followed up her Oscar-winning performance.

Perhaps the plot—a cold-blooded hit man (Hopper) becomes obsessed with his conceptual-artist target (Foster)—looked more mainstream on paper than the cool, elliptic, and arty thriller that Hopper delivered. Or perhaps Jodie Foster, a child in the sixties, just couldn't resist working with one of that decade's culture heroes, who also was a critically lauded director, and the film, shot in New Mexico where Hopper lived, was simply part of her continuing on-location education. In any case, whatever commercial aspirations there were for *Backtrack* disappeared when its distributor, Vestron, a high flyer in the financially overheated mideighties, went bankrupt.

Still, Jodie clearly liked Dennis, calling him a "doll to work with . . . an incredible mixture of an old soul and a little kid. He's been around forever, yet he has this naughty little boy aspect to him. And I think he's really attractive, sexy."[26]

That the feeling was mutual is obvious from the way the director filmed his young leading lady. The chemistry shows on screen.

In several scenes Foster is photographed wearing only a spaghetti-strap silk chemise, and she bares her breasts stepping out of a shower. There's even a kinky sex-play interchange with Hopper.

"Let me tell you something about men," says her character to her transfixed hit-man captor as she slips on a garter belt and stockings. "They have no imagination."

Despite a trite, contrived ending that undermines the wit and style of what went before, this is a picture that deserved wider notice.

FOSTER PLAYS successful west Los Angeles conceptual artist Anne Benton, whose medium is light-emitting diodes and neon signs that—instead of unscrolling the latest stock quotations

or, perhaps, the time and weather—convey cryptic and fragmen-
tary messages, such as IT'S IMPORTANT TO STAY CLEAN/ON ALL
LEVELS, LACK OF CHARISMA/CAN BE FATAL, and MURDER HAS ITS
SENSUAL SIDE. In her trendy Venice gallery, those LED constructs
go for twenty-thousand dollars and up.

After her red Mustang convertible blows a tire on the freeway,
permed-blond Anne, whose dress billows up Marilyn Monroe
style when she gets out of her car, witnesses a mob murder in a
nearby refinery. Later, one of the killers, the mob's Beverly Hills
lawyer (Dean Stockwell), turns up in the police station where she
is being offered protection by a Justice Department prosecutor
(Fred Ward). Anne flees in disguise.

The mobsters—who in addition to Stockwell and Vincent
Price, their godfather, include Joe Pesci and John Turturro—call
in Milo (Hopper), an artistically inclined hit man who aspires to
play sax like Charlie Parker, is partial to the apocalyptic art of
Hieronymous Bosch, and sprinkles his taciturn remarks with
(make that, *wid*) *deses* and *doses*. Inevitably he becomes obsessed
with Anne, particularly after rifling through her abandoned apartment and finding Polaroid snapshots of her in sexy black lingerie
straight out of the Victoria's Secret catalog—a black-lace bustier-
like bodysuit, garter belt, long gloves, silk stockings, and the
inevitable spike heels.

In montage, time passes. Behind an auburn wig, pink lipstick,
and green contacts, the Seattle copywriter turning out clever
advertising copy is really Anne Benton, still missing after two
months. Back in Los Angeles, as Milo turns the pages of a magazine (it appears to be an issue of *Vanity Fair* that actually profiled Jodie Foster, one of the picture's many in-jokes), his eye is
caught by the words in a two-page lipstick ad:

PROTECT ME . . . FROM WHAT I WANT.

Says Milo: "Dat's wanna hers." And he sets off in pursuit,
eventually tracking Anne all the way to New Mexico, where she's
a blue-eyed blond again, all good bones, fine angles, and tawny
skin.

Milo surreptitiously watches her shower, then he kidnaps her. And it's at this point, about two-thirds of the way through, that the picture goes wrong, giving justification to the critics, activists, and others who were beginning to accuse Foster of "always" playing victims.

Earlier the movie's been stylish, witty, and entertaining. For example, while mobsters commit murder at Anne's apartment and the white-collar neighbors are plainly visible through their window smoking crack in the background, the police, sirens wailing, arrive to arrest . . . four male Hispanics, just passing through. References to art, literature, and jazz abound; even D. H. Lawrence himself, portrayed in cameo by cult director Alex Cox (*Repo Man, Sid and Nancy*), turns up in a surreal fiesta scene.

Each shot of the first two-thirds of the film seems composed with care and an almost academic sensibility. Then, as happens all too often in Hollywood, there's a preposterous third act, betraying what's gone before and apparently tacked on.

Anne, who at first rails against the existentialist hit man who's violated her, calling him "not only . . . a murderer and a rapist, but . . . a pompous fucking asshole," falls in love with Milo. Maybe it's that literal and not-so-silent lamb, stuck in a crevice in one of the picture's most shameless in-jokes, that he helps her save.

Until he's got her in handcuffs and, later, when he forces her to put on her sexy lingerie for him, Anne is a self-possessed artist/businesswoman, mixing a take-charge facade with girlish vulnerability, and with more than a passing resemblance to Jodie Foster herself.

Says Anne of herself in a radio interview, heard as she drives down the freeway during the opening credits: "I use language and construct texts as the content of my work. My ideas come out of literature as much as anything else. In fact, I've deliberately avoided the subject matter of art altogether."

But once he's got her into her dominatrix manqué getup, Milo gets so excited leering and nuzzling her that he resorts to a maniacal *Blue Velvet* shtick, Hopper's memorable and much-imitated crazed gasping-in-lust noise:

UNH! UNH! UNH!

Jodie as Anne, in garter belt and sheer black stockings, leaning against a small table with her head thrown back and one leg hooked over Milo's shoulder, looks as if she's about to burst out with a laugh.

THE MOVIE, with its impressive ensemble cast, which also included Bob Dylan and Charlie Sheen in cameos (as a chainsaw-wielding artist and as the pizza-munching boyfriend, respectively), disappeared into cable, even vanishing from some listings of Foster's films.

Observers of Foster's career could easily assume that she was about to fall back into the pattern of the early and mideighties, when she'd acted in a succession of failed films, ambitious pictures mostly, with excellent ensemble casts and weak scripts marbled by artistic or literary pretensions.

Though there was to be no theatrical *Backtrack*, that didn't herald the career backtrack that seemed to confound so many Oscar winners. Foster remained publicly stoic and philosophical: "It's not like I've had the most successful career in the world. . . . I haven't. I've had a lot of ups and downs and movies that made no money and hard times and all of that. And I will continue to."[27]

Ahead for Jodie Foster, though, was the shoal of yet another bankrupt Hollywood company, another controversial commercial and critical success, more subterranean whispers and not-so-subterranean threats, a second acting Oscar, and the achievement of an ambition she'd been pointing toward for more than half her life.

WHIZ KID REDUX

SHE WAS JUST FOURTEEN when she confided to Andy Warhol, during a lunch-hour interview at New York's Pierre hotel, that what she really wanted to do when she grew up was direct, and she was all of fifteen when she wrote and directed *Hands of Time*, a short film included in the Time-Life/BBC documentary *Americans*.

From then on, to the interviewers' inevitable what-do-you-want-to-be question, the whiz-kid actress who had once unhesitatingly answered, "President of the United States," might reply: A serious actress . . . or a writer . . . or a teacher . . . or—with a sly, tongue-in-cheek nod to her most famous child-actress predecessor—an ambassador. But being a film director was the option to which ever after she would return.

"I know enough technically," she opined at the age of twenty-three in a studio biography in words that sound as if they might have been written for her (a common practice in such publicity-department-generated documents) but which she nonetheless would have approved. "I would start perhaps with an intimate film."

In her midtwenties she'd narrowed her professional ambitions down to two—writing fiction and directing. Of the former she said, shrewdly assessing the demands of the blank page, that she felt too "roving for that now, a little too fickle."[1]

When it came to directing, however, her consideration was purely tactical, that of an aspiring general, a veteran of many hard-fought campaigns, considering a first command: "The thing is to know what you want and to be able to get it from people twice your age. . . . I can't afford to do a half-assed job."[2]

For years she'd also disparaged awards, saying it was the work, not the acclaim, that mattered. But with the new acclaim, she realized, came new clout.

Winning the Academy Award as Best Actress "means that projects that could not get done now get done because you say you want to do it," she said a few months after Hollywood's big night.[3]

"The whiz kid," she added, sounding as if she was already thinking ahead to the Scott Frank script that had been floating around Hollywood, unmade, for years, "that's definitely going to be a theme in my work."

But even headstrong ex–whiz kids who find themselves, after years of diligence, finally atop the greasy pole may find they have to contend with a chorus of nay-saying advisers urging caution. Foster did.

"Nobody wanted me to direct a movie right after I had won an Academy Award," she said. "It was like, 'Come on, go out, get some performances, this is your big chance.'

"And it all made sense. But sometimes you have to do things that make sense for you. It wasn't so much a career thing, but I loved this piece.

"I had to save Fred. You know like, 'Am I going to let some other director do this?' "[4]

Any list of Jodie Foster's favorite directors would include François Truffaut, Louis Malle, Jean-Luc Godard, Woody Allen, John Sayles, Nicolas Roeg, Alan Rudolph, and Stephen Frears. She had always liked *Franny and Zooey*, too, J. D. Salinger's delicate short novel about whiz-kid siblings growing up, trying to be real and true and to overcome the abundant temptations of "phoniness" while coming to terms with their extraordinary backgrounds and family. It struck in her an obvious chord.

The story—actually two related tales: "Franny," a short story, and "Zooey," a novella—focuses on two of the seven precocious Glass children, and the longer second part, "Zooey," is ostensibly narrated by Zooey's older brother, Buddy, a writer.

All seven of the Glass children in their turn had appeared on a radio program, "It's a Wise Child." "Off and on, during their broadcasting years, all seven of the children had been fair game for the kind of child psychologist or professional educator who takes a special interest in extra-precocious children. In this cause, or service, Zooey had been, of all the Glasses, hands down, the most voraciously examined, interviewed, and poked at."[5] No wonder that, at the time of the narrative of his eponymously named story, Zooey, now a young adult, has turned to acting.

No wonder then that when Jodie Foster turned to directing as a young adult, the story that she picked had a distinctly Salingeresque feel.

THE STORY OF *Little Man Tate* would fit right in to the Glass family chronicles. Fred Tate (Adam Hann-Byrd), the seven-year-old "little man" of the title, is a little boy with a big intellect, a soulful demeanor, and a sensitive stomach, who's being raised by a single working-class mother, Dede (played by Foster).

Dede, a tough-talking brunette with an auburn tint, smokes and drinks. When she's not working, she wears big hoop earrings and long, shapeless cotton print skirts with thrift-store T-shirts. She adores her son, and we see her fixing him his favorite meal (French toast and fried apples), dancing a joyous, impromptu jitterbug with him ("Care to cut a rug, handsome?" she says, swinging him happily into the air), and assuring him that his father's identity is unimportant because actually he's the immaculate conception.

"That's a pretty big responsibility," sighs solemn Fred.

Little Fred balances his mother's checkbook, writes music, and paints pictures for her. He takes her phone apart just to see what makes it work and worries about everything—from the disease that "turns a little kid into an old man" to a *USA Today* headline he glimpses in a newspaper box: MOTHER EARTH MELTDOWN, the headline fairly screams, *Can the Planet Handle Humanity?*

"Oh my God!" Fred exclaims as Dede pulls him away. Like Ella Fitzgerald's elegant version of Cole Porter's "I Get a Kick Out of You," which plays over the opening credits, and the jazzy swing-era big-band source music counterpointing Mozart and Brahms on the soundtrack, it's one of the picture's many Woody Allen–like touches.

(Source music, as its name implies, is music emanating from a particular source in a scene, such as a radio or phonograph, while underscore is usually mood music played under dialogue or action.)

Not surprisingly, Fred also has an ulcer. He wakes up fearful in the middle of the night and regularly dreams himself into the middle of a van Gogh painting. At school he's bored; the other kids tease him. "All I want is someone to eat lunch with," he says wistfully.

He comes to the attention of Doctor Jane Grierson (Dianne Wiest), director of an institute for gifted children, whose assistant, Garth (played by David Hyde-Pierce, a regular on TV's "Frasier," who's billed in this presitcom role as just David Pierce), describes the seven-year-old second-grader to her:

"He writes poetry. Paints in both oils and water. Plays the

piano at competition level. All the while maintaining what appear to be unlimited skills in math and physics. Can't explain it, Jane," Garth adds, his voice taking on a quiet note of wonderment. "It's not so much what he knows, but . . . what he understands."

Reluctantly, down-to-earth Dede, a struggling waitress in a Chinese restaurant, risks losing her son by giving him the opportunity to excel at Grierson's institute for gifted children. She even accedes when Doctor Jane takes Fred away for a summer at college, where he can live in Grierson's rural Virginia mansion while she studies him for a proposed book.

At an Odyssey of the Mind math contest, Fred gets his first appreciative glimmer of the benefits of being "special" and in the spotlight. In a smooth and subtle scene Fred is applauded as he answers one math puzzler after another.

"What's the cube root of 3,796,466?" asks the off-screen moderator.

"One hundred and fifty-six," Fred replies, his usually tense and solemn features brightening into a shy smile as he notices that pretty little girls in the audience are impressed and clapping.

It's one of the many smooth directorial touches in a film that never calls attention to its cuts or camera angles unless there's a narrative or character-defining point being made:

A quick cut to Fred standing by himself at the far end of a long hallway nicely emphasizes his loneliness.

Neon-blue animation, sparingly used, illustrates the kinesthetic nature of his gift. Watching a game in a pool hall, for example, he can see the blue vector and trajectory lines of the clacking balls.

TATE DEBUTED IN October 1991, the last picture released as its distributor was going into bankruptcy, to generally adoring reviews for both Foster the director and Foster the actor. Typical was the enthusiasm of the veteran show business trade paper reviewer, who enthused that "first-time director Jodie Foster has presented a stirring and magnificent portrait of the human spirit" in which, "with a supremely sensitive eye toward the boy's terrifying limbo-like childhood, [she] conveys the terrible horror of being an aberration in everyone's eyes." As Dede Tate, the "earthy and erratic mother," Foster the actor was simply "wonderful."[6]

The role of Dede Tate is "more of a step than anything I've done in a long time," she said, "because I show more something I've never before chosen to show on screen. And that is: totally warm, totally loving. I feel like I've built my characters on this strength stuff, and now I want to explore a part of me that's a little bit lighter, but not necessarily comic."[7]

The parallels between single-mother Dede Tate and her gifted child and single-mother Brandy Foster and *her* gifted child were both obvious and much remarked on during the picture's publicity buildup—not that Foster was at ease with this obvious publicity hook, denying any autobiographical intentions at every opportunity.

"Well, okay, I was an actor and I was young and I was pretty good at it, but I don't consider myself some kind of prodigy," she said.[8]

"Everyone I grew up with was a single-parent kid," she also allowed. "All my mom's friends were divorced women, and they would sit around and talk about that asshole and that bastard, whatever."[9]

"I wanted to do a film that reflected me," Jodie said on another occasion, "spoke of the things I cared about, but none of this is autobiographical or anything. . . . The single-parent thing is such a huge part of American life. It's definitely been my entire life."[10]

Three elements had attracted her to the script, she said, which had been circulated around Hollywood and passed over for years until she read it. "The single-parent thing. It's the portrait of an artist and it's about a misfit. . . .

"They're all misfits. Dede because she refuses to be conventional, Dianne's character [Doctor Grierson] because she is tragically bereft [of emotions]. My favorite idea is that in trying to create a world where he fits in, [Fred, the whiz-kid seven-year-old] creates a world for the misfits around him. It is not a quest for conventional happiness."[11]

Perhaps not conventional, but a quest nonetheless, and one aiming for what any good sixties child would consider the highest of all holy grails—self-transformation. Foster could wax lyrical about her movie's seven-year-old eponymous hero:

"He's absolutely my hero and the herald of a new age. He's somebody who, by virtue of being born of the imagination of these two women, will go on and become an amazing man. He will be not only a rocket scientist, but a great trumpet player, too; not only somebody who is respected, but who is a great kisser."[12]

With Foster at the helm, the picture had shot for ten weeks in mid-1990 in Cincinnati, where she told a news conference at the beginning of the shoot that directing was "sort of all I thought about when I was younger. It was a much more meticulously technical industry then, so I grew up thinking I got applause when I stood on my mark, when I moved into focus."

While Foster was declaring her intention to "be a role model for the certain things I believe in," reporters, even local Ohio-based ones, presumably not privy to the hottest dish at Le Dôme, the posh show-business restaurant on Sunset Boulevard, were increasingly alluding to her "too-good-to-be-true image [that] may come from a desire to squash the potential for any unfair rumors."[13]

Unfair rumors?

Newspaper and magazine readers could easily skip right past those kinds of vague nudges, especially because they were invariably buried by the overwhelmingly positive depictions of Foster actually *being* that on-set role model—acting, directing; always focused on her vision of the way things should be, but never overbearing or less than collegial; even cooking for the cast and crew. On her crew jacket were the initials *BLT*, for Bossy Little Thing.

"To have a vision," she said, "you have to have a large ego. . . . You have to love being in that position where 35 people are asking 20 questions and you pick one."[14]

Too good she may have seemed, but by every account the set she ran was a happy place, no doubt because Foster knew the difference between making decisions and throwing tantrums and because of the blue-collar camaraderie she tried to embody. "I love being a director in the camera car," she enthused. "You're outside, you have to wear a hat, it's windy, and your eyes tear and you've got headphones on and you're sunburned.

"You feel like you're actually working, it's more of a blue-collar experience. . . . I have a bad Protestant work ethic; I don't feel like I'm working unless I'm working."[15]

"You get up at six in the morning," she said another time, making it sound as if it were the most bracing and beneficial thing in the world, "and it's like a blue-collar job—all the idiots that sit at the Polo Lounge don't mean anything. . . . That's what fascinates me when people talk about the film business—they're talking about people who sit in suits and go to lunch, but that's not what it is."[16]

Foster thrived as a director, calling it the "most sane, and healthy experience I've ever had. . . . I've just never been so happy. When I got back home [after the day's shoot], I'd cook soups, and I'd watch the news, and I'd actually read books. . . . I was tired, but I could have gone on and done another movie three weeks later."[17]

Unlike directing, she added, acting was a "tremendous strain. It is tiring to have to have your whole job be about pleasing someone else—pleasing the lighting guy, pleasing the audience. And then also maintaining the character of the character. It's just exhausting. Much more exhausting than directing."[18]

Being behind the camera and in front of it at the same time was "just tiring," she said afterward. "It's two different heads that are constantly combating. One's very analytical, very focused and structural, always being the observer and the choice-maker. The other side has to be free of that. Acting is a very freeing kind of thing; you have to forget about structure, to be able to just be open."[19]

She herself had only one regret about the experience of directing her own film, Foster told a magazine writer visiting the set, and it was the "only thing I've ever regretted in my whole life."[20] While directing her debut picture, she'd started smoking cigarettes again, Merits. "I quit for many years," said the actress known since her childhood for her throaty voice, "and then I started directing this movie.

"I get nervous. And I'm not stupid, and I'll never do that again. I was such a fervent nonsmoker for so long." (Like many another fervent nonsmoker, though, she'd cadged the occasional cigarette on the side: a few years back, on the *Five Corners* shoot, she'd puffed away . . . but only surreptitiously, outside her mother's presence.)

Meanwhile, back in Hollywood, Foster announced a "two-year, first-look agreement with Orion Pictures to star in, direct and produce motion pictures."[21]

A "first look" is just that: a studio typically offers money and/or a combination of services, which could range from office space and secretarial help to film marketing and distribution, in return for the right of first bid and the right to match any subsequent better offers.

The Oscar winner could have had her pick of deals and studios but chose relatively small Orion, she said, because of the hands-off faith Orion execs had demonstrated in the Jonathan Demme movie she'd just finished.

"Orion didn't interfere at all, where there are a lot of people that would have liked to make that [film] into something which would have been less risky and much less interesting," she said, adding that once *Tate* was wrapped she looked forward to "broadening her repertoire," perhaps to doing comedies or "something that's really romantic and sensual."[22]

Soon, though, Jodie Foster was shuttling between a Los Angeles editing room, where she was putting the finishing touches on *Little Man Tate*, and New York City, where she was reshooting scenes in *Shadows and Fog*, a new movie directed by Woody Allen (also an Orion auteur), when she formally announced the formation of her own production company.

The company was formed within the terms of her original first-look deal, and its first hire, president of production Carol Bahoric, called her new boss a "voracious intellect" who "reads all the time." Her job, Bahoric added, is "to constantly feed [Jodie] material."[23]

Of course as the nineties began, Orion, the perfect home for *real* filmmakers and the "grand exception"[24] to the corporate studio culture, found itself caught in the same financial shakeout that was squeezing the other smaller Hollywood production companies that had thrived in the eighties. The company had a cable network "output" deal, obligating it to provide ten or twelve pictures per year to Showtime. With the company's once forceful and farsighted original leadership either aging or heading for the exits or both (and at the second level generally perceived as weak), a grab bag of forgettable titles was being put into production, just to meet the terms of that cable deal, by the company that once had made *Amadeus* (the Best Picture of 1984), *Platoon* (the Best Picture of 1986), and *Dances with Wolves* (the Best Picture of 1990).

Production costs were soaring past projected budgets; marketing and distribution costs in Hollywood were ticking past $10 million for the average theatrical release, affecting all but the biggest players with the deepest pockets. The company was scores and scores of millions of dollars in debt and falling further into the red with each new movie. At Orion, just making the interest payments to its bankers and creditors became ever more onerous. The company found itself with approximately a dozen movies at or near completion, including *Blue Sky* starring Jessica Lange and Tommy Lee Jones, but without the advertising and distribution millions necessary to "open" them.

With drastically depleted resources, Orion's executives were forced to choose between releasing a Jodie Foster–Anthony Hopkins picture and releasing their Jessica Lange–Tommy Lee Jones film. They rolled the dice with the former, but they were desperate for immediate extra dollars so that by the time the awards and accolades started coming in, they'd already consigned it to an extraordinarily early exposure on home video, releasing it in October 1991 to capitalize on the larger market for "horror pictures" around Halloween. *Blue Sky*, a flawed film featuring its own bravura performances by the two leads, didn't see the light of day until mid-1994.

Just to raise cash, the company's desperate officers took an approximately $8 million loss on a nearly completed picture by selling Paramount Pictures the rights to it. The movie, which went on to take in $113 million at the box office, was *The Addams Family*. If Orion's panicky management had only held on to that one picture, said analysts with the luxury of hindsight (and with box-office grosses in hand), the company might have pulled through.

Abruptly, with its debt load crunching toward $1 billion, bankruptcy for Orion, the company that had always invested in individual filmmakers, was near, and in December 1991 the company filed for Chapter 11 protection. Among its unsecured creditors: Jodie Foster, Kevin Costner, and Jonathan Demme.

Meanwhile, the whiz kid was now reading every "green light" script in town, searching for good material, but because this was Hollywood it would be three years before her new company's first production made it to the nation's movie screens. In the meantime, there was another, final Orion movie to launch, the one that she'd shot before directing *Little Man Tate*, and another Academy Awards show to attend.

THE SILENCE AND THE SHOUTING

FOR ONCE, JODIE
Foster had misjudged her impact in a part.

Of course, to misjudge a movie entire is easy. There is such a mazey obstacle course between the page and the celluloid unspooling in a darkened theater, so many opportunities for even a strong-willed and intelligent actor to lose everything (that most movies shoot out of narrative order may be emblematic of the whole process), that it's rare enough to hold on even to the nuances that make a good character. It was one reason she could still shine in a misbegotten farrago: Jodie Foster, consummate pro and A student, learned her characters cold.

Of this character, Clarice Starling, an ambitious young FBI agent, she said: "She's a rural person who's desperately trying to become an urban person . . . someone who has a fear of the mediocre, [a] fear of being average."[1] She was also another in the long line of Jodie Foster characters who had been raised without a father figure, this time a heroic cop killed in the line of duty.

Of course, in classical mythology the hero often is fatherless, even parentless, and in making the mythic heroic journey essentially gives birth to himself. None of this was lost on former Yale literature student Jodie Foster, who took to repeating a précis of the archetypical hero myth as part of her PR repertoire for the picture. "She's a hero because she has tragic flaws. She faces things about herself that are ugly, and while facing them she solves the crime."[2] Never had a female character in cinema been allowed to enact the mythic journey, the hero's progress, she rightly declared.

But Foster seemingly mistook completely the potential *impact* of the trainee FBI agent she was playing in *The Silence of the Lambs.*

Referring to Faye Dunaway's climactic revelation at the end of *Chinatown,* she said, "It's not a flashy part, not the Oscar kind of part where you say, 'My sister, my daughter, my sister, my daughter.' But I don't make movies for flashy, juicy performances. I have to find something in the story that's part of my progress, part of this little train I'm on. In order for me to spend three months on something, to understand it, it has to speak to me personally."[3]

Soon, though, other voices were speaking to her personally. Outrage by vocal and media-savvy gay groups greeted the picture from the start.

If, after all the awards and the industry approbation, looking back the rage now seems somewhat misplaced, then—at the start of the second decade of the AIDS epidemic—with the media fearful of fundamentalist backlash and all too quick to resort to easy negative gay stereotypes, particularly when sketching villains, it was understandable nonetheless.

In the early nineties, on recession-plagued network television, threatened boycotts by fundamentalists and other visceral opponents were driving advertisers away from gay-themed episodes of prime-time series and costing the broadcasters millions. Prestige projects such as *And the Band Played On* had languished for years in development limbo. Mincing "fairies" were still a staple of stand-up comedy and late-night TV monologues. *Basic Instinct*, too, with its "lesbian psycho-killer" (as its protesters often referred to Sharon Stone's bisexual character), was in the offing, and the gay and lesbian media-watch hotline in L.A. was buzzing with anonymous tips from agents, studio executives, and other self-styled insiders about alleged homophobic slurs in early versions of its script.

Activist groups, such as Act Up and Queer Nation, retaliated with a tactic known as "outing," that is, publicly exposing prominent closeted gays and lesbians.

(The ethics of outing divided the gay community, and eventually the practice subsided; but its morality aside, in Hollywood, where image is everything and almost anyone who has achieved any prominence will be whispered about, the threat of exposure was particularly effective. Around this time, and not coincidentally, the Hollywood-based entertainment industry took significant steps toward eliminating institutionalized gender-based discrimination—recognizing, for example, same-sex partners for the purposes of insurance and other benefits.)

Because gays and lesbians had long assumed that Jodie Foster was one of their own (without any confirmation from her), her participation in a film that brought an effeminate cross-dressing villain to the screen was at the time considered a special betrayal. And her continued silence on the subject of her private life in general and of her own sexuality in particular was regarded as careerist cowardice rather than as the principled stand of a proper young woman. Then, too, there was the unseen shadow of the past:

John Hinckley may have been long forgotten by the public, but as recently as December 1992 the director of the Secret Service called him a "security threat" and administrators of the hospital where he remains incarcerated to this day attested that he was a danger to himself and others.[4] And unknown to all but her own circles, Foster was still taking precautions against wanna-bes, some of whose yowlings continue to echo from the far reaches of cyberspace.

Naturally she didn't talk publicly about any of this, even while the *Silence* controversy gathered momentum. Her response post-Hinckley had been not to talk about it. More than just wishing the crazed copycats away, the tactic did turn down the spotlight that focused their dangerous, irrational hostility. Now, faced with new hostility from activists passionate about their life-and-death cause, she adopted the same tactic—a "principled" silence—though this time whatever danger existed was arguably to her career alone. Ironically, Foster the Oscar winner became embroiled in the controversy because of a role for which she wasn't even the first choice.

The Silence of the Lambs, directed by Jonathan Demme from a screenplay by Ted Tally based on the bestselling Thomas Harris novel, is an expertly crafted thriller, both a procedural and an epic psychological contest of wills between its two main characters—Hannibal Lecter (Anthony Hopkins), a mad serial-killing psychiatrist in a cage, nicknamed Hannibal the Cannibal by the tabloid press, and Starling, an ambitious rookie FBI agent.

(*Silence* wasn't the first time Foster and Hopkins had signed to do a picture together. A decade before, in 1981, they'd come within weeks of filming in Austria on *The Beethoven Secret*, with British director Ken Russell and a cast that included Glenda Jackson and Charlotte Rampling. "Preproduction was in an advanced state," according to a trade paper report, "and the cast, including Foster, was assembled when interim financing from West Germany fell through, thus shuttering the venture."[5])

Starling is desperate to succeed on this her first assignment: a ticking-deadline manhunt for a second mad killer, luridly known in the tabloids as Buffalo Bill, who skins his female victims. Hannibal the Cannibal had already made his screen debut in another thriller, *Manhunter*, directed by Michael Mann and based on *Red Dragon*, an earlier Harris novel. Clearly this was a narrative that could have lent itself easily to a slasher B-picture treatment, complete with hapless, screaming coeds in their lingerie fleeing the knife-wielding psycho.

Director Demme had first offered the part of Clarice to actress

Michelle Pfeiffer. But after reading the script, she turned it down, "unable to come to terms with the over-powering darkness of the piece," said Demme,[6] who'd also directed Pfeiffer in *Married to the Mob*, for which she'd received generally excellent notices.

Foster, though, could look into the heart of that same darkness and recognize herself.

"I play very dire human situations, survival situations," she told one writer of her instinctive career choices. "I love getting to that place of seeing things that people don't ever get to see, and experiencing that. It's like somebody who is a fighter pilot or who deals with crippled children—they like that, too. That's what fuels me."[7]

"To tell you the truth," she said on another occasion, "I would have crawled over broken glass for the role—wearing shorts."[8]

Said her *Silence* director, "This is the first part Jodie has played, that I know of, where she hasn't had to mask her intelligence . . . where she's allowed to be every bit as smart as the exceptionally bright person she actually is."[9]

It may have helped to have a director like Demme, as collegially minded as she, who readily accepted her insights into the character of Clarice, as well as, in Anthony Hopkins, a costar with equally stellar acting skills, whose own insights into the subtext of Clarice's character made for one the most electrifying—and unscripted—moments in *The Silence of the Lambs*.

It was in a crucially important scene, when young trainee Clarice, in her tasteful, no-nonsense business dress, first meets the sadistic Doctor Lecter, who stands, head back, waiting for her at the center of his subterranean cage, seemingly sniffing some faint air current, a predator sensing his prey.

She wears Evian skin cream, he tells her, and sometimes L'Air du Temps. "Good bag and cheap shoes," Lecter sneers. "You look like a rube . . . with a little taste. . . . You're no more than one generation from poor white trash, are you, Agent Starling?"

Their sparring makes for a high-stakes drama of seduction and manipulation, and in a lapidary moment that wasn't in the script

Lecter begins to imitate Clarice's carefully camouflaged country accent. That trace of accent is the dead giveaway of this proud and proficient young woman's humble origins.

"That wasn't in the script. Tears came to my eyes," Foster told one interviewer. "It was so hurtful. As an actress, I was thinking, 'This guy's making fun of my accent!' It was a moment where the boundary got very fuzzy between me and Clarice."[10]

"The first time he did it," Foster recalled another time, "I wanted to cry or smack him. I just was so upset. You're in a scene, so you sort of feel those things, but as an actor, having somebody imitate your accent—it just killed me. It was the perfect thing for Lecter to do, because Clarice has been hiding her rural accent, trying to speak better, escape her origins in a certain way. And here's a guy who nails her."[11]

Lecter even knows what Clarice loves most in the world, and he tells her so.

"What is that, Doctor?" the young agent cries out in her dramatic distress.

"Advancement, of course," the cunning madman replies.

The obvious professional admiration Foster felt for her costar was mutual. Said Hopkins of another moment in the same scene, when Lecter suddenly hisses at Clarice and, in a tiny facial gesture, Foster recoils: "She works with such economy. She doesn't do a thing, and yet you can see all the thoughts going through her eyes, like 'Oh, my God, this man is an animal, a beast.' And I think that's the great skill of an actress like Jodie—it just shows on her face; she doesn't have to act it."[12]

The verdict of both her peers and the press was that act she did, and they gave her the awards that proved it. The public responded, too, making *Silence* the third-highest-grossing movie of the year. By the time of the 1992 Oscar telecast, *The Silence of the Lambs* had a worldwide theatrical box-office gross of approximately $245 million. It was too late for Orion, though. The money went to clamoring creditors, while the company staggered into bankruptcy court.

Traditionally, the crowded Hollywood movie awards season begins with the Hollywood Foreign Press Association's Golden Globes in January and ends with the Oscars in late March or early April.

The HFPA, with fewer than 100 members, had once been the object of ridicule, assumed to be composed of part-time stringers for obscure publications in tiny countries beneath Tinseltown's imperial notice. The standard joke of the time was that on the night of the Golden Globes getting good service in a fine restaurant was impossible because all the waiters were gone— moonlighting as members of the HFPA. Throughout most of its first half-century of existence, and particularly in the seventies and early eighties, the Globes were widely thought to be for sale to whoever wined and dined the most members of the foreign press.

But lucrative award-show TV rights and the practice of incorporating the Globes into movie marketing strategies and publicity campaigns, as well as the belated discovery that the international film marketplace was a booming growth center, had changed all that by the time Jodie Foster stepped backstage in early '92, her Golden Globe for Best Actress in a Drama clutched in one hand. The Globes, combining old-style shameless Hollywood puffery with lifestyles-of-the-rich-and-famous entertainment journalism and TV-era visibility, had become one of the best-attended shows of the entire award season and a treat for celebrity watchers. With its voting procedures and membership requirements no longer murky, the HFPA is now courted more assiduously than ever, the Globes now the much-ballyhooed precursor to the Oscars.

Jodie Foster, educated, widely traveled, and multilingual, had been a favorite of this group for years, and on this night, with a red AIDS-awareness ribbon pinned to a curvy black dress that showed plenty of décolletage, she looked every inch the American film goddess of fevered, movie-mad foreign imaginings.

Stepping before the microphone and facing the TV cameras,

the jostling paparazzi, and the adoring foreign press, she laughed brightly and a little nervously.

"I have a very annoying habit where I can't stop laughing when I get one of these things," she smiled, holding up the Globe statuette. "It's like Robert Redford in *The Candidate*."

She looked around expectantly for a reaction, but the odd little joke, a reference to that film's final scene, flew right past the assembled press.

Unexpectedly on an evening like this, the first question—from Alex Ben Block, editor of *The Hollywood Reporter*, one of the two daily show business trade papers widely read in executive suites (and therefore often reflecting the purely business concerns of its readers rather than artistic matters)—was about the deadly serious business of box office. It sounded like a classic softball, but there was a barb.

"You worked so hard on *Little Man Tate*"—she smiled, obviously grateful for the appreciation, looking down from the raised stage at her questioner—"and it didn't get maybe as much recognition or box office as it ought to." The smile faded, replaced briefly by an incredulous moue, but the editor plunged ahead, noting that *Silence* wasn't as "personal" a picture. "Could you compare them?"

"Gee, well I *really* disagree," she began. "It got more box office than I ever expected, and it certainly has been very, *very* well received."

(It has been, in fact, profitable, costing less than $10 million and grossing upward of $25 million.[13])

"It's a very small movie." She shrugged, tucking a wayward blond strand behind her ear, "and I don't have any bones about *that* certainly, if that's what you're looking for."

If that's what you're looking for. She was a veteran. She knew that real reporters were always looking for *something*, that at best their questions were meant to be provocations, that there could be a simpleminded or sycophantic question, but there was no such thing as an innocent one.

She turned away, back to the TV cameras and the room at large. "I loved *Silence*," she declared with some feeling. "It's a movie that's stuck with me. . . . It's both very complex and very literary, and at the same time great entertainment."

"Were you haunted by it?" immediately asked a voice from her audience.

Her pale blue eyes narrowed, as if she couldn't quite believe the assumption behind the question. After all, this was *moviemaking*, not real life, and she *loved* making movies. "I like doing dramas," she said dryly, "that's what I do, so I enjoyed it."

The next questioner wanted her to compare directing and acting: how much more preparation did directing a movie require than just being in front of the camera?

Again she laughed, amused. "Two more years, I think."

It was a craftsperson's joke, something the crew might chuckle over, setting up on location some late night, but again the black-tie journalists, most of whom covered the beat from a fan's perspective, didn't get it. She forged ahead with an earnest explanation.

"I'm not so sure that its preparation necessarily *is* different, but it's much longer," she reiterated—Hollywood's golden girl, ever the good student, giving a recitation.

"Um, I think I probably look at it the same way I always did acting, which is, um, identifying whatever it is that you're trying to say and then trying to execute it. It's kind of as simple as that: trying to tell a story.

"With directing, because it's sort of the *ultimate* vision, there's a lot more time spent, a lot more energy."

Another journalist from the pack asked, Does winning awards increase the pressure "to top yourself?"

Still grasping the statuette she'd won only moments before, she laughed, pulled back on that persistent fall of hair, and sighed.

"Oh, I dunno," she laughed, "I dunno." She paused. "I try not to think." Again she paused, then began again:

"I try to not *concentrate* so much on what other people think, or what the image is or what I should do," she said, in words that certainly must have reminded her listeners of the rumors and the protests and the swirling controversies. "The *only* reason being," she said with a quick smile, "that every time I've done that, I've made some horrendous mistakes. So I guess in order to detour around those mistakes I've chosen to just kind of like—"

She threw up her hands, her voice dropped to a mock-dramatic whisper:

"*Find something I like*," she said breathily, in a sly parody of the stereotypical movie-star answer, adding in her usual, no-nonsense Val-gal voice, "and do that, and that usually seems to be the safest bet."

The brief backstage press conference was winding down. Would there be a sequel to *The Silence of the Lambs?*

"Sure, why not. But nobody's heard anything," she said, although by then all the expense-account lunchtime talk was of a hopeless rights tangle, with veteran Italian producer Dino De Laurentiis holding fast to the sequel rights, Universal Pictures chairman Tom Pollock contending that he had a verbal commitment from De Laurentiis to a sequel deal that would split the cost of acquiring the sequel novel and producing the sequel picture between De Laurentiis and Universal, and novelist Thomas Harris at work on a sequel but adamantly opposed to including De Laurentiis in any future production. Within a month of the Globes, the dispute between De Laurentiis and Pollock, who ironically was De Laurentiis's former lawyer, had resulted in a lawsuit, followed by a countersuit less than two months later.[14] To date, of course, all parties have maintained their dogged *Silence* sequel silence.

The final long-winded question, about the "strong heroine" she'd played in *Silence*, was not just a softball, but a *slow-motion* softball that gave Foster the opportunity to repeat what she'd said to innumerable interviewers during the movie's publicity push. To be sure, it was condensed and warmed-over Joseph Campbell, the scholar of comparative mythology who'd been hip young Hollywood's favorite learned academic reference ever since George Lucas first cited his *The Hero with a Thousand Faces* and the "mono-myth" of the hero's progression as an inspiration for the *Star Wars* saga, but it was true:

"Mythologically, in terms of the movies," she began, improvising the tiniest variations on a speech she knew by rote, "I think it's the first time that women have really had access to that myth—to a real folklore connection to what a hero is—meaning, you know, you're born in a village"—she extended her arms in parallel in a pedagogic gesture, emphasizing each step of the progression with forceful two-handed stabs, quite unlike the subtle moves with which she shaded her on-screen characterizations:

"You leave to find what's ailing [its people]—you know, the plague—and you go in [to the unknown] and run against gnomes and demons and yourself—and all sorts of fears you have—and finally, when you understand them, you can slay the dragon and bring the panacea back home, and never, *ever*"—her eyes narrowed in emphasis—"be a [simple] citizen again.

"That's the traditional myth that women have never been allowed to have." Here she shifted her weight from side to side, the good student finally fidgeting as she came to the end of her declamation. "So I think it's a big step. Thank you so much." And with a wave she was gone.

But in that awards season, it wasn't the last time Jodie Foster would face the cameras and microphones of the entertainment press, nor was it the last time they would hear her recite the progress of the hero.

When next she recited the hero's progress before the same chorus, it would turn out to be an extraordinarily emotional public moment in a most guarded and private life, and it would go completely unremarked.

Was it because the men and women who cover show business and Hollywood on a daily basis are so jaded that they didn't react when Jodie Foster nearly broke down in front of them, or was it because the sudden show of genuine emotion and vulnerability didn't fit their preconceived notions of her image—and that they are so much a part of the system of show-business-as-usual that Tinseltown's carefully constructed images are all that they allow to creep into their reality?

It could be simply that the moment passed so swiftly and that the occasion was no more than a glorified photo opportunity. In other words, it wasn't the story that they were there for, so when the unexpectedly newsworthy happened they didn't recognize it as a story at all.

When it came to being nominated for and winning awards, *The Silence of the Lambs* broke most of the rules. Despite the skill with which it was executed, it belonged to a genre—the horror picture—that was dismissed more often than lauded. Also, in a clever marketing ploy, it had been released on Valentine's Day 1991, more than a year before the Academy Awards for which it was eligible, and the conventional wisdom was that invariably only films released late in the calendar year are given serious academy consideration.

In fact, in the previous two decades only two films released early in the calendar year—*The Godfather* and *Annie Hall*—had been named Best Picture.

But Foster was right about the picture's classic structure; it aroused terror and pity and moved audiences. Despite its unlikely release date, it remained memorable months later.

In addition to its innate artistic merits, other factors kept it in academy members' minds: A clever Orion Pictures marketing campaign featured mass mailings of boxed editions of the *Silence* videotape. The cable TV window put the picture into academy homes as industry attention was turning to Oscar. And finally, the arrest of serial killer Jeffrey Dahmer in the summer of that year was a most chilling real-life reminder of its gruesome subject matter.

Its outraged opponents couldn't forget the picture either. From the beginning, gay activists protesting Hollywood's portrayals (and lack thereof) of gay men and women in general, and the portrayal of the effeminate *Silence* serial killer specifically, pointed their protests directly at Jodie Foster. To general skepticism, the filmmakers responded that the villain was not in fact gay.

Outweek, a gay publication at the forefront of the "outing" movement, proceeded to make Foster a regular target, threatening to "uncloset" her if she didn't label herself a lesbian and declare her solidarity with the movement.[15]

In the most egregious example of the outing phenomenon, within days after the movie's release, posters went up in lower Manhattan with her picture and the following caption: "Oscar Winner. Yale Graduate. Ex–Disney Moppet. Dyke."[16]

The perpetrators of the poster campaign turned out to be an anonymous graphic designer and his equally anonymous lover, an editor, who apparently had acted independently of even the most militant of the gay organizations, according to the *Village Voice*. Targeted, too, was former talk show host, game show mogul, and hotelier Merv Griffin; in both cases the posters bore a headline that parodied the Absolut vodka advertising campaign logo: "ABSOLUTELY QUEER."

Among the gay and lesbian population of Greenwich Village, as elsewhere, the tactic was controversial, often drawing sympathy for Foster and ire at this violation of her privacy, and even setting off a debate in the pages of the *Village Voice* about the propriety of outing a celebrity.

After articles about the poster campaign, which referred only to a "former daytime perennial" and a "famous young actress," another columnist indignantly defended the practice of outing the celebrities, saying about his own colleagues that "they want to collaborate on making gayness the skanky secret it's always been— unreportable, unspeakable, except with the nod of approval from the star. Next time they write something about a famous person that some prejudiced reader might find unflattering, I hope they'll ask permission first."[17]

The debate and the controversy continued to rage, and as the Oscars approached, gay organizations raised the specter of confrontation and disruption. Implicitly—and sometimes explicitly—coupled with the threats was an offer that amounted to blackmail: if Jodie Foster came out, on Oscar day they'd stay home.

Of course, ironically, the last time the Oscars had been disrupted was when John Hinckley shot Ronald Reagan, hoping to win Jodie Foster's love.

More than ever, the Academy Awards was primarily a television show, one of the most watched on the planet and big business on a par with such annual televised pop culture rites as the Super Bowl. And like the Super Bowl, the Oscars had developed their own drum-beating rituals leading up to the big event. One was a photo opportunity par excellence.

About a month before the big show, the nominees assembled, often at the local Beverly Hilton hotel (owned by Merv Griffin, as it happened), where they faced the paparazzi and the press. The *celebrity* nominees, that is.

Like the home audience, which was presumed to be uninterested in the scientific and technical awards and most of the craft awards, the entertainment press couldn't be bothered with any but famous faces, who posed for a group photo, commemorating their Oscar "class." Those actors and actors (and star directors) up for the very "biggest" of the academy's awards usually were prevailed on by the army of attendant publicists to take a few questions.

Jodie Foster showed up that day in an elegant jacket the color of absinthe over a light lemon-green silk shirt that set off her blue-eyed, blond beauty. She seemed in a jolly good mood, recognizing press people she knew from other events.

The first query was from a woman, asking the how-does-it-feel question: "How does it *feel* to be nominated for an Oscar again?"

"Every time it's different," said Jodie Foster, harking all the way back to the midseventies and *Taxi Driver*. "The first one, I was very young and it was all these grown-ups and I knew that it was a complete fluke and that I would be looking for a job very soon, so I didn't really take it very seriously. It was just like this big Disneyland ride. . . .

"The second one is finally realizing that, I guess, you're a member of the industry, which—I dunno, I guess I'd always considered myself being on the outside of that.

"Well, this is very different and bigger in a weird way," she said, running a hand through her hair, "because the whole movie has been totally embraced. You know, there are so many pieces to a film. There's the acting part, there's the tone of the movie, there's the sort of visual style. . . . [There's] the emotional impact that a film has, there's emotional levels, intellectual levels, entertainment levels. . . . I really do think that *Silence* is one of those very rare films that accomplishes greatness in kind of every single area."

"Jodie!" Even before she'd finished her remark, from the side of the press pack crowded in front of the small stage with its blue Oscar-curtain backdrop came a man's voice, urgent. "Many are predicting your movie will sweep the Oscars."

Hands clasped behind her back, she turned to him, rolling her eyes heavenward and smiling, as if the very idea was too absurd. "I don't know about that," she interjected brightly, rocking back and forth on her heels as the questioner, who now had her attention, bored in on her, insistent, from an unexpected direction:

"They are protesting your movie—"

She nodded vigorously. "Hm." The muscles around her mouth tightened.

"—and its portrayal of a gay character."

Again, a vigorous nod, a curt "Hm."

"Any response to the possibility of gay groups like Act Up and Queer Nation disrupting the Oscars?"

Short and simple. On the one hand it strains credulity to think she really didn't expect some such question. After all, the Academy Awards television show, with its billion or so viewers in countries all around the globe, made a tempting target for any activist looking to seize the world's spotlight, and there was nothing to suggest that in that year those particular groups, in their rage against AIDS and homophobic prejudice, weren't deadly serious about their threats.

On the other hand, Jodie Foster, with literally a lifetime's experience in its workings, knew the Hollywood publicity machine well, and she knew its unwritten codes of conduct. In the equation among celebrities, almost all with their own publicists, and the "beat" reporters, whether for print or television, who regularly covered them, the power had long since flowed *away* from the press. Press agents demanded—and got—what once would have been unheard of or rightly regarded as scandalous: quid pro quos, such as guaranteed magazine covers and a veto over who was assigned to the story, in return for making their stars available.

Because of Hinckley, Foster herself was a pioneer in the art of the circumscribed public appearance. At least as far back as *The Accused,* her representatives had been demanding magazine covers and getting them. Under such straitened circumstances, pointed questions were widely regarded—even among the reporters themselves, who might have been expected to ask them—as the equivalent of bad manners, and anyone with the temerity to ask risked being banned from the Hollywood trough.

In this atmosphere even a bad review sometimes was enough to get a film critic banned from a studio's lot. If, for example, a reporter noticed that a star's filmography had been altered to remove an early and controversial role and had the bad grace to raise the issue to the star in an interview or at a press conference, the punishment might be exile from future studio press junkets.

(A junket brings together movie reviewers and writers from all around the country, usually in Los Angeles or New York, where they are wined, dined, shown a preview of an upcoming film, and allowed to interview its stars, usually in a group setting. Until recent years studios paid all expenses for such trips; now many of the larger and more reputable publications pay travel and hotel expenses for their entertainment writers.)

Any response to the possibility of gay groups like Act Up and Queer Nation disrupting the Oscars?

For just a fraction of an instant Jodie Foster looked shocked.

"No, not really," she said blandly. On her face she fixed a look that hadn't been seen on screen since the tough-kid roles of her early preteen days:

Wide-eyed, with raised eyebrows, it was an expression of *who, me?* disbelief; it was the same look of bland innocence Audrey, accused of shoplifting, had affected in *Alice Doesn't Live Here Anymore*, the exact same what's-he-talking-about? reaction with which hard-case Casey in *Candleshoe* had responded when being read her "rap sheet." But her complexion was suffusing with a rosy flush.

"Next," said Jodie Foster. She turned away from the questioner, turning to the other side of the room.

There was drama in the air, certainly, but no acknowledgment of it or any follow-up. It wasn't as if the other reporters didn't know what the questioner had been talking about or what his pointed query implied. They'd all been hearing the rumors for years, and this was the kind of tidbit they'd take back to their newsrooms and editing bays, chuckle over, and dine out on for days. Instead, David Sheehan, a genial and laconic entertainment reporter who is a Los Angeles local TV fixture, proceeded to ask, droningly, if she would "talk a little about" her "identification" with "heroic victims."

"Yes," said Jodie, an oddly needy and nakedly grateful smile flickering across her face while he went on with the lengthy preamble to his question. Looking ostentatiously fascinated, as if she was hearing the question for the first, and not the hundred-and-first, time, Jodie Foster tried to take a deep breath, but it came out sounding audibly shallow and strained.

Incredibly, she was rattled, still flushed, and for just an instant it looked as if right there, right in front of the TV cameras, she might burst into tears.

As she tried to unspool her standard answer, her normally confident and clear voice came out even deeper and fuzzier, strangled-sounding and brimming with emotion. She virtually forced the familiar words out.

"Well, ah, one of the major attractions of the film, I think, is initially—the initial attraction, and what, uh—"

Her voice seemed to be emanating from somewhere behind her eyes. She ran a hand through her hair, steadying herself with the familiar gesture.

"—is new about the film is that it's the first time, uh, in film history, I think, where you have a true female hero.

"In that way, it's a hero that follows that kind of folklore mythology. It follows that structure."

Catching her breath, she swallowed.

"There's, ah, a horrible disease that, ah, is killing the people, the young warrior goes out into the forest of experience and meets gnomes and demons and, um, sort of mythic horrors and fears."

Now she was warming to the lines; visibly, her emotion was subsiding, her familiar public persona returning.

"And by understanding her own fears and smallness and her own, um, impossibilities and lack of potential—"

Her voice caught, but she continued on, almost through it: "—she finally finds the dragon, slays it, gets the, um, panacea, brings it back to the village. Where she no longer belongs."

She took a deep breath. "And, and, that structure, that sort of folktale structure, has never been given to a woman before unless she had some sort of, you know, steroid version of a male hero or, in the other sense, a woman running around in her underwear, who's actually more of a victim than a hero."

"One more question," one of the hovering publicists quickly called out.

It was another of the how-do-you-feel questions, this time with phrasing about the award-season "clock" ticking down.

It was as if it had never happened. Jodie Foster went from genuine relief to relieved performance, responding to the lengthy question with a suave look of mock horror.

"Oh, *that* clock," she deadpanned to general laughter from the press. "I was getting scared there for a moment. . . ."

But the real moment had ticked past unnoticed. Once again, Jodie Foster had risen to the occasion, maintaining her composure, albeit by a hairbreadth.

She answered expansively: "It's been said a million times that the nomination is everything. . . ."

Of the possibility of actually winning the Oscar lottery, she shrugged, "I'm not that attached to it." When she stepped away from the microphone, Barbra Streisand followed her onto the stage.

The disruptions and large-scale protests threatened for the Academy Awards that year never materialized.

There may have been a few more "serious" protesters sprinkled among the movie-mad fans, the buxom "starlets," the bearded transvestites in high drag, and the hollow-eyed zealots holding aloft their "You'll burn in hell" and "Repent, sinners" signs. But they amounted to only a few more than the usual number of colorful extras on the far fringes of the big TV show.

The Silence of the Lambs swept the major categories.

Orion Pictures' post-Oscar party, held at the posh downtown Los Angeles restaurant Rex Il Ristorante, "exuded opulence, from the five-foot-high ice rendering of the 'Lambs' insignia to the free-flowing champagne and menu of lobster, salmon—and roast lamb."[18] Arbiters of style saluted it, but financial analysts churlishly called the party an example of the excess that had led to the company's financial downfall.

Jodie Foster steadfastly maintained her own silence about her private life, and the tabloids, which at the height of the pre-Oscar outing craze had staked out her house in the San Fernando Valley, finally gave it up.

When she won her second Best Actress award, Jodie Foster said: "I'd like to dedicate this award to all the women who came before, who never had the chances I've had, and the survivors, and the pioneers, and the outcasts . . . and to all the people in this industry who have respected my choices and not been afraid of the power and the dignity that entitled me to. . . . Thanks to the academy for embracing such an incredibly strong and beautiful feminist hero that I'm so proud of."

Backstage after winning, wearing a bone-white, kimono-length Armani jacket, decorated with the de rigueur red AIDS-awareness ribbon, over beaded champagne silk pants and a matching blouse the color of beaten gold, and clutching the statuette in a white-satin-gloved hand, the thirty-year-old actress again was on top of the film world. Again, she stood in front of the royal blue stage curtain decorated by images of the Oscar statuette. This time a silently flickering monitor, tuned to the ceremony live, flickered on a nearby stand. This night there would be no pointed questions.

Asked if she felt happy or hysterical, she laughed giddily. "It's an incredible thrill. It's a little bit different, because the whole film was taken into consideration."

The next question—"What's the picture done for the women's movement?"—gave her a chance to repeat, almost verbatim, her speech about the hero myth and to reiterate that feminism was humanism.

Did she have a "door" into Clarice? she was asked. Jodie laughed.

"Is that one of those Juilliard words I don't know?" she asked in teasing good humor. The rejoinder, perhaps subconsciously, harked back to her *Accused* costar Kelly McGillis and to what Jodie had said about her during the period when the rumors about them were first sweeping Hollywood: professionally she was Foster's antithesis; the Juilliard-trained actress who not only was able to cry on cue but could specify which eye.

"Uh-oh, I knew this was gonna come back to haunt me," she added jokingly. If it was a taunt, there was no one in the Academy Awards pressroom to take her up on it. "Well, I think the password really is that she is compelled," she continued. "She is compelled the same way that Hannibal Lecter is compelled.

"Human beings find what their psychological agenda is. Your life and your work is about figuring out what it is you were meant to do . . . and hers was an incredible, neurotic in some ways, agenda of saving women, the women who are common, the women who were forgotten and were, um—"

"Turn around!"

A shout from the back of the pressroom interrupted her eloquent observations.

"*Turn around!*"

The trouper's instinct was to continue: "—and were always cast aside—"

"Turn around! It *won!*"

She turned to the monitor with its live "feed" from the auditorium: *The Silence of the Lambs* was just being named Best Picture of the Year, giving it Oscar's equivalent of the Grand Slam.

A look of pure and unaffected delight suffused Jodie Foster's face. Instinctively she bent as if to leap cheerleaderlike into the air.

"NO *WAY!* " she shouted out, stomping the ground emphatically. She straightened instantly, pushing her hair back and turning back to the microphone. ". . . Only two other films in history that've ever done that," she trilled, excited. "*I can't believe it!*"

There were other, brief questions that night.

"I think protest is good," she replied with another of her standard, albeit accurate, formulations to one circumspect question. "It's American, not against the law. . . . Criticism helps people learn . . . but anything else falls into the category of undignified."

Asked about the future, the young actress, still glowing with happiness, explained that her fantasy was to go away now and sit in a hot bath "for four days" and that, while she would never give up acting, "directing has more to do with my real personality."

She then was called away for a quick still-photo shoot with "Tony" Hopkins.

But if this had been a movie and not real life (and despite all the surface glitter and the behind-the-scenes stagecraft and management, life is what it was), her story would end on this freeze frame:

NO *WAY*!

Jodie Foster triumphant.

HOLLYWOOD'S
MAVERICK

ON THE SAME DAY
in October 1992 that Orion Pictures, the "mini-major" where she had first hatched her Egg Pictures production company and under whose aegis she'd made her directorial debut and won her second Best Actress Oscar, emerged from bankruptcy, Jodie Foster announced a three-year production deal with Polygram Filmed Entertainment.

PFE was the newly formed film production and distribution division of Polygram, the giant London-based music company, which in turn was 80-percent owned by Philips, the Dutch electronics conglomerate. By early 1995, PFE was responsible for approximately 10 percent of its parent company's revenues.[1]

Its titles included a number of ambitious small movies with poor to moderate box-office performance, including *Posse, California, Romeo Is Bleeding, Shallow Grave,* and *The Adventures of Priscilla, Queen of the Desert.* The company's greatest success story to date has been *Four Weddings and a Funeral,* a $4.5 million romantic comedy, nominated for Best Picture, that was on its way to grossing $250 million worldwide.

PFE, specializing in small-budget films for the international marketplace, had been building its presence in the all-important North American marketplace through deals with semiautonomous, artist-oriented production labels, including Propaganda, Working Title, Interscope, and Foster's Egg. Given PFE's reputation for being (within fairly stringent budgetary limits) director-friendly and its international connections, it was a natural for Foster, who more than a decade before had had one of her best-regarded teenage roles in *Foxes,* a film produced by PFE's predecessor, Polygram Pictures.

The new deal, which gave her the coveted power to "greenlight" up to six of her own Polygram-financed pictures (within the usual agreed-on cost/revenue-projection limitations), with a reported total production budget of as much as $120 million dollars, with tens of millions more available for marketing, instantly vaulted her to the front ranks of Hollywood women and made her arguably the most powerful female actor in show business.

Under the terms of the deal, if she "controlled" material, then she was "exclusive" to PFE; if she didn't control—that is, if she was an actor or director for hire in a film—she was free to go anywhere.

The deal, she told a showbiz trade paper, gave her "more control over my destiny. . . . I want signature films. And the costs will be appropriate to what the picture is. I've always been driven by material, not price."[2]

In Hollywood such "indie-prod" agreements, securing the services, exclusive or otherwise, of prominent or "à la mode" actors as independent producers, are announced with numbing fanfare and disturbing regularity. Most such pacts in practice are actually only so-called housekeeping deals, in which the touted money securing the producer manqué's services is spent on lavish offices, paychecks for the entourage, and other vanity and status items.

Foster's own Egg office, on the other hand, didn't live up to the palatial standards of most of her indie-prod peers. (At least one veteran Hollywood producer, for example, is cared for by a full-time, in-office liveried butler.) Designed by her sister Connie, Foster's was spacious, casual, computerized (with a Mac LCIII); "self-referential memorabilia is kept at a minimum."[3]

In the same trade paper announcement, Polygram Filmed Entertainment's president observed, correctly, that "if you look around at all the studio lots, there's a lot of money thrown at these independent producers which goes into paying huge overhead and by the end of the day there's nothing left to make movies." Not so with Jodie Foster.

Egg Pictures' housekeeping expenses—its overhead—was drawn from a fund separate from the money that financed the pictures she wanted to make. And that both signaled her seriousness as a production player and gave her additional clout.

Foster followed up *Tate* and *Silence* with the release of *Sommersby*, a poignant story that had all the tragic inevitability of the classic Homeric myths she so appreciated. The picture, filmed entirely on location in Virginia, was set in a small, ravaged village in post–Civil War Tennessee.

Costarring Richard Gere and directed by Jon Amiel, the picture was an expert transliteration of the brilliantly told and beautifully photographed 1982 French film, *The Return of Martin Guerre*, which took place in Europe in the sixteenth century. (The *Sommersby* script was by Nicholas Meyer and Sarah Kernochan, from a story by Meyer and Anthony Shaffer.)

It was a coproduction involving Le Studio Canal+, a French production company that would have looked favorably on the casting of Jodie Foster, fluent in French and bankable in Gaul from the 1976 Cannes Film Festival on. Gere himself was one of *Sommersby*'s two executive producers.

Both *Guerre* and *Sommersby* tell essentially the same story: after many years away at war a man returns to a small village, claiming to be a beautiful young woman's long-lost husband. Though she does not believe that the man who has come back from the war is her husband, nonetheless she falls in love with him. In a climactic trial he can save himself from death only by renouncing his new identity and his new life.

Although partisans of *Martin Guerre* expected a Hollywood fiasco, *Sommersby*, with solid performances by its two leads, turned out to be a well-crafted romantic melodrama. Yet again Foster's reviews were better than those of the movie itself. Said one reviewer: "She is memorable . . . managing to project a combination of sweetness, fire and mature beauty that is impossible to resist."[4]

AFTER SIX YEARS Jack Sommersby (Gere) has returned to the barren and bedraggled village of Vine Hill, Tennessee, its houses ransacked by the victorious Yankees and its land played out and useless for planting cotton.

"Ain't nothin' leff here but hard ground an' nobody to work it," says a dispirited local woman, joining an impromptu procession of joyous villagers accompanying their returning Jack as he treks to the big house where his wife Laurel (Foster), wearing a caped greatcoat and mannish hat, both the brown color of the newly turned earth, her blond hair worn over one shoulder in a long, loose braid, is scything the overgrown field in front of her columned antebellum house.

A lad sent from the town warns her that her long-lost husband has returned from the war. Quickly she gathers up her son, Robert, changing into her burgundy finery, her hair gathered into a wine-red crocheted snood, to greet Sommersby on her doorstep.

Jack Sommersby greets the boy, then, looking down shyly, softly takes Laurel's hand. "I'd forgotten how beautiful you were," he whispers, glancing up as she looks down.

They embrace. On her face is the tiniest suggestion of a knowing smile. With the Greek chorus of villagers ratifying their reunion with clapping and *oohs* and *aahs*, the merest flutter of her eyes tells of her misgivings.

As Jodie Foster plays her, Laurel Sommersby is a woman making calculations while brimming with barely checked emotions. She *wants* this man to be her husband but knows on some level that he is not.

For one thing, this Jack Sommersby is not a drunken wastrel, nor is he the lout who ignored his wife, unless it was to abuse her, for the three years they were married before he went off to the war.

This Jack Sommersby is a gentle lover who reads Homer to Robert and conceives of a plan to revive the town. And he's no bigot either.

That night, at a feast honoring the returning prodigal, when he offers food to a group of blacks who've come to pay their respects, the villagers have their first hint that *this* Jack Sommersby may not be the *real* Jack Sommersby.

Laurel, moving through the festivities, watches warily, but she's pleased despite her misgivings. Soon they bring the town together in the seasonal work of planting and harvesting a new crop— tobacco.

Eventually this strong southern woman accepts her new Jack Sommersby, both in her heart and in her bed. With the verdant crop coming in, the town is reborn, and she gives birth to a daughter, too.

But on the christening day Jack Sommersby is arrested for murder and taken away to Nashville. Laurel and many of the townsfolk form a caravan of wagons and carriages to travel with Sommersby to his trial.

Only by confessing that the man with whom she's been living is not her true husband can Laurel keep Sommersby from the gallows, but he'd rather die as the honorable Sommersby than live as "Yellow" Horace Townsend, the coward he'd once been.

On the verge of a mistrial, he dismisses his attorney and cross-examines Laurel himself. At first she won't be dissuaded; after all, she's trying to save the man she loves.

"God, you are a hardheaded woman, Laurel," he says, his voice rising with exasperation.

"And you are a stubborn idiot," she shoots back from the stand. Foster's voice drops to that trademark husky whisper. "You are not Jack Sommersby, so why do you keep goin' on pretending that you are?"

Angrily, he shouts. "How do you know I'm not?"

"I know because—"

Again, louder, he goads her. "How do you know, Laurel?"

"I know because—"

"HOW DO YOU KNOW?"

"I know because I never loved him"—her voice decelerates abruptly, descending between breaths to the softest, most tender of emotion-filled confidences—"the way that I love you."

For the merest instant Laurel seems stunned by what she's just said. It's a powerful moment, expertly realized by two actors at the top of their game, one that was shown repeatedly in the film's advertising campaign, but it's not Foster's most emotional speech in *Sommersby*.

That comes shortly afterward, in a jail cell, as "Jack" awaits the final walk to the gallows. He takes comfort from the fine price the town's crop has fetched and explains how he came to take the place of Jack Sommersby and why he can't go back to his former identity.

As he is about to take Laurel in his arms, she pulls back.

"You want to hold me, then you hold me today and every day after that." Foster's voice, so expert at conveying just barely checked emotions, pitches to near hysteria. "You say that you love me? Then you show me! You be a father and you grow old with me. That's what love is."

From where do actors' emotions arise? How biographically shall we interpret their choices? Here, in this moment of this film, the temptation to picture that remarkably alert and precociously intelligent youngest child of the single mother and the absent father is irresistible.

THE STORY OF *Sommersby,* Jodie Foster said repeatedly on the day she "did media" for the movie is "about unconventional people struggling with a very conventional and confusing time."

Of Laurel and her transformation from hopelessness to strength, Foster said: "That's a pretty fiery journey for a woman living in [that] conventional time."[5]

Less than two months after *Sommersby* opened, Foster made another appearance at the Oscar show. For this ultimate industry event the reigning Best Actress, there to ratify presentation of the tiara to her successor, came in traditional character—the glamorous film goddess. As one fashion commentator put it:

"Super svelte Jodie Foster strolled in looking like a classic 1950s movie star . . . [in] a sexy Armani strapless black gown featuring a tucked bodice, swirling side panels and a rosette belt."[6]

After the benighted quasi-art movies of the eighties, Foster was now in a deliciously paradoxical position, uniquely occupying a cusp between ultimate outsider, a serious actor/artiste with sights credibly fixed higher than the bottom line and goals loftier than those of crass commercialism, and ultimate movie-business insider, a big-bucks producer with the financial clout to bring her projects, exactly the way she wanted them, to the big screen.

She could finally act in her Woody Allen film, *Shadows and Fog,* but it was a small role in one of the Manhattan maestro's least successful pictures. (Not surprisingly, the reviews for her brief turn as a hooker were better than those of the picture itself.) Once, she'd considered it a badge of professional honor never to have appeared in a summer blockbuster. Now there was *Maverick.*

At the height of the *Silence* shouting, Jodie Foster, in her auteur role, said that the movie she wanted to direct after *Little Man Tate* would be about no less fundamental a subject than sex. "I want to make a movie about . . . my generation and sexuality. It's about time people had frank movies where sexuality is treated really honestly, where women are sexual people instead of constantly being on some nonsexual pedestal."[7]

Although a Jodie Foster–directed film about that particular subject should have partisans lining up expectantly at movie theaters, that such a movie wasn't her very next project and hasn't happened yet may be a disappointment but shouldn't be a surprise. Movie ideas float around Hollywood for years—Oliver Stone's *Platoon*, for example, was a decade in development; the *Forrest Gump* story circulated around the studios for nine years—and they regularly metamorphose, gaining and losing "bankable" elements (to cite just one of many examples: before a rewrite, *Beverly Hills Cop* had been designed for Sylvester Stallone).

In fact, mentioning "wish list" ideas in the press, especially in the Hollywood trade papers, is a time-honored industry method of drawing attention—and dollars—to a project. No sooner does an actor develop "heat" than he or she turns up "attached" to one or another movie that may or may not ever get made. From *Iris* on, whenever her career was in the ascendant, Foster would turn up in these kind of read-between-the-lines trade stories. For example, just days before she won her second Academy Award, a trade paper article had her "prepping" a picture called *The Bum*, a "love story between a newly separated Malibu housewife and a beach bum, in which the actress hopes to star later this year."[8]

For savvy trade paper aficionados, in that short *Bum* story the word *hopes* and the caveat, near the end, that neither Foster nor her agent could be "reached for comment" suggest that the entire article was merely a signal, probably from the would-be picture's producer to the actress herself or to other potential "elements."

About a year later a number of trade papers had Foster in *Trackdown*, a Chunnel disaster movie, as an American "engineer battling to prevent a train accident in the rail link between England and France. The project is one of several Chunnel-based action films."[9] None of the touted projects ever saw the proverbial light, and Foster has yet to don her engineering hard hat.

Signaling the industry was a game that Foster, through Egg, played as well. According to a 1993 trade paper story,[10] the first Egg project would be either *Jonathan Wild*, a $20 million period crime melodrama set in eighteenth-century London and directed by Neil Jordan (*The Crying Game, Interview with the Vampire*), or a biography of sixties actress Jean Seberg in which Foster would star.

In announcing the biography of the actress best known as costar of Jean-Luc Godard's classic New Wave picture, *Breathless*, Foster explained, in language that sounds as if it's taken directly from a press release, that "it's the relentless searcher in Jean that fascinates me. That quality led her into situations and events I personally have protected myself from. . . . It seems that she was desperately torn between the public and the private self, the icon and the unformed small-town girl, the expectations and the reality."[11]

Maverick, too, was most likely a signal, a message from Jodie Foster to the Hollywood powers-that-in-perpetuity-be:

The team could count on her—the insider's outsider—alternating her future "signature" Egg pictures with big-budget, big-studio, high-concept omelets.

It was for all intents and purposes the Eastwood strategy, modeled after that other box-office heavyweight who had used his acting clout in commercial pictures, particularly the *Dirty Harry* series, to produce, direct, and act in smaller, more heartfelt films, pictures such as *Bronco Billy* and *White Hunter, Black Heart*.

By alternating the commercial blockbusters with the more personal pictures, Clint Eastwood maintained both his autonomy and his box-office appeal, eventually melding the two streams in his career in the multi-award-winning *Unforgiven*.

In show business the acronym *NATO* stands for a powerful organization, but it conjures up images of uniformed ushers ripping tickets rather than of soldiers guarding frontiers. The National Association of Theatre Owners, at its annual ShowEast convention, held in 1994 at Atlantic City's Trump Taj Mahal, named Jodie Foster the recipient of the George Eastman Award, recognizing her "enormous contribution to the industry as an actress, director and producer."

She received the award almost two years to the day after the original announcement of the Polygram deal (like many another film star, Jodie Foster had repeatedly bemoaned the lack of good scripts in general and good roles for women in particular) and almost two months before the premiere of *Nell*, the first Egg picture to make it to the big screen.

Jodie Foster, cinephile that she was, readily conceded that when she went into a video store she'd usually seen every movie in the drama section but not one of the comedies. Her mother, Brandy, who'd done so much to form her daughter's taste in movies, was the first to remark that Jodie had a talent for comedy, but it was almost two decades after she first publicly said so that audiences got a chance to judge for themselves.

The picture, a $40 million summer "event" blockbuster, was *Maverick*, pairing her with Mel Gibson and his *Lethal Weapon* series director, Richard Donner. For appearing in this frothy package Foster reportedly was paid $5 million, doubling her previous high fee. (By comparison, Demi Moore's fee for acting in *Strip Tease*, a high-profile picture based on the novel of the same name, is reported to be $10 to $12 million.)

To the cognoscenti of the Hollywood cocktail chorus, Foster in *Maverick* was as if Katharine Hepburn had turned up in *The Treasure of the Sierra Madre*, but to hear Foster herself tell it the decision was easy:

"They sent [the script] to me on a Thursday. . . . I read it on Thursday afternoon, said yes on Friday, and had costume fittings on Saturday. I said, 'Yeah, I can't wait to start . . . and don't change a thing!' "[12]

Once again, though, she'd been a second choice: actress Meg Ryan (*Prelude to a Kiss*, *I.Q.*) had been Gibson and Donner's first pick to play Annabelle, the southern-belle cardsharp who beats Maverick at his own game, just as Paul Newman was first on their wish list for the role James Garner was to play. But with a new baby at home, Ryan passed.

Despite that, despite the fact that the William Goldman script she'd so admired soon gave way to improv on an alarming scale, and despite the Gibson/Donner good-ol'-boys-at-play gonzo style, Foster got right down to it, improvising a pratfall in her first scene that set the entire tone—propriety mixed with klutziness—for her character.

"This is what I realized about comedy," Foster reflected after it was all over. "The truth about comedy is that it doesn't matter how it looks, it doesn't matter how it cuts, doesn't matter what they're wearing, doesn't matter if it makes sense. That only thing that matters is if there's a spark."[13]

And when it came to the all-important relationship with her costar and his favorite director, that spark certainly was there.

Said Donner, who'd originally opposed her casting: "She's really sexy and cute and fun, hell, she's a darling little thing."[14]

(His remark may have been an inside joke. For years Foster had noted rather proudly that her friends called her BLT, for Bossy Little Thing, as well as Miss Authoritiva.)

The Darling Little Thing initially received Donner's old-style directing instructions on the *Maverick* shoot with something akin to offended professional propriety. "If I was in a drama and in the middle of a scene, and he said, 'Turn right! Open your mouth! Hurry!' maybe I would want to kill him. But it's actually right for what we're doing."[15]

Stories at the time touted the unlikely blossoming friendship between the very proper Miss Foster and the backslapping Mad Mel, who were said to have remained close long after the *Maverick* shoot was over. (In fact the actor turned up at the December 1994 premiere of *Nell*, her first produced picture under the Polygram deal.)

That relationship, and even the simple fact that Foster was acting in a picture with Gibson, once again raised the ire of many gay people, activists and others, who considered the actor a homophobe (as well as an ingrate, given how many gay men had mentored his career and were in his professional circle) for widely reported disparaging remarks he'd once made in a Mexican publication about gay men, remarks that he later recanted. Despite her long and consistent silence on matters private, to say nothing of matters sexual, and despite the absence of any corroboration whatsoever, gay activists, as a matter of course, had claimed Foster as one of their own for years, and they held her to their own pointed standards. (Gossip has its own gospel, of the urban-folklore sort, and the "common wisdom" and the testimony of "friends of friends" is usually enough to render such a verdict.)

But *Maverick* wasn't the first time that innuendo had surrounded Foster and a leading man. In *Sommersby* the performances of the two costars had to overcome the persistent snickers of Hollywood wags who've dogged Richard Gere's career with rumors that he, too, is covertly gay.

Foster's comparison of the two leading men, subtext or not, is still informative:

"I can't think of two more opposite people thrust in the same position: handsome men who every time a woman walks in, she responds to them in a really positive way.

"Richard is somehow completely internal; he doesn't notice anything that's happening around him. And then occasionally he'll put his high beams on you, and you feel like the most special person in the world because he just allowed you to come in for a moment. People die for that; they go over like dominoes.

"Whereas Mel is so unaware of himself, all he does is spend time doing magic tricks for people, or trying to think of things that will make them squeal, or disgust them. He listens in a way that's kind of innocent, and he disarms you because he's so unthreatening—he's like your best buddy immediately. . . .

"Richard feels very . . . dangerous, like a spiderweb you could get stuck in. . . . Mel's a kid."[16]

While a year after *Silence* swept the Oscars Foster still would talk about private habits and public threats in only the most general ways, Gere had learned to be direct about the rumors regarding his habits in the bedroom, declaring, "I don't give a fuck what people think about if I'm gay or not."[17]

When it came to Jodie Foster and her sexuality, the press had long spoken a language that all but the cognoscenti might not fully understand.

In the May 1994 issue of *Vanity Fair* Michael Shnayerson's profile is an excellent example of the read-between-the-lines genre. Calling her "famously guarded about her personal life," the writer asks the subject of his piece, mock prosecutorial style, "Is there anything, Miss Foster, you wish to say on the subject of relationships at this time?"

"Nope," she replies, adding that a private personal life is more important to her than "feeding the curiosity machine."

Calling her reticence "irksome in a way," the writer nonetheless finds "something marvelous" about Foster's ability to have never "disclosed a romance" or been "photographed with a beau."

Of course, in alluding to a "beau," or boyfriend, the writer was being disingenuous. True or not, there is by now no one left in the entertainment press who doesn't share the same, probably simplistic, conviction about her sexuality.

And for almost the first time in her adult career, it surfaced directly—no allusive reportorial coyness—in a profile that appeared in the *Los Angeles Times Magazine.* In remarking about Foster's "enormous defenses," the writer points out that for years Foster had threatened to walk out on interviews if "certain topics" were raised. One, of course, was John Hinckley's assassination attempt. "Her other hot-button question—rumors of lesbianism."[18]

With the closet door open and the issue finally in the room, Foster reacted with aplomb . . . and characteristic reserve. She denied ever having threatened to walk out on a "print" interview (probably an accurate distinction: her cancellation of a "Good Morning America" interview after the producer wouldn't accede to her requirement that Hinckley not be mentioned was, after all, not a walk-out, nor was the interview for print; the same is true of her cancellation of a "Today" interview during her *Little Man Tate* promotions after being told Hinckley would be mentioned in her introduction).

Then the actress, who between movie assignments often went to Paris (the sophisticated City of Light also is known for turning down the heat when it comes to intrusions on personal privacy), added, "I don't really care what people will say. This is an American phenomenon, that people think that they interact with a celebrity by hearing them talk about pain, so they think they know them. I think that's bullshit."[19]

Of course she was right. By "talk about pain," we can assume she meant expose her innermost being generally. But after all, she was in the Hollywood image business—and broadly construed, that meant, as she knew better than most, not just moviemaking but publicity shaping as well, even though for some time she'd been chafing at all publicity image-making, her self-created Ivy League overachiever persona included.

"There's a reason it's my image," she conceded after winning her second Oscar. "That's the side of me that I show journalists. I really like talking about my work and thinking it through. So I don't think my image is erroneous. But what's funny is that . . . my work on screen is actually becoming more emotionally accessible."[20]

Yet in her company's first picture she stars as a backwoods orphan who communicates through her own self-created language, which the film's other characters and the audience have to learn to decipher.

But decipher it they do. The first Egg Pictures picture, a $22 million production, is a Foster tour de force. From the day it was officially announced as a PFE and Twentieth Century Fox coproduction to its premiere at the motion picture academy's own Samuel Goldwyn Theater in Beverly Hills, which she attended escorted by a Fox executive,[21] almost exactly one year passed. But months before its debut the publicity drumbeat for a third acting Oscar had begun.

And when the nation's film critics finally got a look at *Nell*, they almost unanimously agreed that it was another acting triumph for the star, although they split on the merits of the melodramatic story itself.

Because Foster produced, and because the picture was so transparently a star vehicle, critics rightly blamed her for the *Nell* story's sentimental or formulaic "Hollywood" touches, particularly the final courtroom scene, which many critics disparaged, regarding it, typically, as a "bow to commercial pressure . . . [that] doesn't invalidate what has gone before, but . . . does reduce the movie's effectiveness."[22]

(Foster's response, on more than one occasion, to the "star vehicle" criticism was to call the movie a "three-handed piece" and to say, "I can name the forty different clichés, the flashy clichés, I could have played, but decided not to.")

A *New York Times* critic articulated a larger complaint, noting that, because the producer/star was, like the character, a "free-spirited woman who dances to her own secret music. . . . [Foster's] independence has been impressive enough to suggest that 'Nell' . . . would be subtler and riskier than ordinary fare. . . . What's remarkable is how seldom it delivers [on that promise]."[23]

Nell will certainly deliver on its prime mover's other promise—the bottom-line one. Even before her Best Actress nomination, which was certain to boost its theatrical take, the movie had grossed more than $30 million at North American theaters, a performance that, according to the show business trade papers, was on the good side of "moderate."

Nell was directed by Michael Apted (the *28 Up* documentary series, *Coal Miner's Daughter*, *Gorillas in the Mist*, *Blink*) from a script by William Nicholson and Mark Handley, based on Handley's original play *Idioglossia*—a word meaning "one's own or a separate language."

Of the fifty-four-day location shoot Apted said, "I never directed a director before, but Jodie never second-guessed me. It was a no-nonsense atmosphere. There was absolutely no Hollywood b.s."[24]

NELL (FOSTER) IS a young Appalachian woman, speaking a unique and impenetrable language, who is discovered alone in a remote cabin by Jerome Lovell (Liam Neeson), the local doctor, after the death of her hermit mother.

Nell is innocent of electricity, running water, processed foods (preparing for the role, Foster lost a dozen pounds on a macrobioticlike diet), and the rest of the modern world. She fears men and goes outdoors only in the night hours.

We first meet her as an expressively keening voice over the opening credits, then as a bony hand gently placing daisies over her dead mother's eyes.

When the doctor arrives with the sheriff, they find Nell cowering in the rafters, and the doctor discovers a scrawled note in the old woman's Bible: "The Lord led you here, stranger," it reads in a cramped hand. "Guard my Nell."

"Officially that creature does not exist," the sheriff tells Lovell after trying to discover who Nell is. All he comes up with is an old newspaper clipping about the long-ago rape of Nell's mother as she returned home from church.

Soon, though, Nell does have an official existence: she comes to the attention of Paula Olsen (Natasha Richardson), a psychologist in Charlotte, the nearest city, where the scientific establishment is thrilled at the possibility of putting a genuine "wild child" under the microscope and addressing such basic questions as "Where do gender roles come from?"

Indeed. And because this is a Jodie Foster movie, it addresses other, by now familiar questions: What constitutes a family?

What's the relationship between being "special" and being "normal"?

And how can anyone, much less a feral individual, live a semblance of a private life in an Oprah- and Geraldo-dominated world?

Nell's traumatic and terrifying relationship with the press, which hounds her with flashbulbs and helicopter rotors, too, echoes her incarnator's.

As one of the Charlotte behaviorists, foreshadowing Nell's inevitable discovery by the outside world, puts it: "Nell will find she's hired a lawyer, an agent and three bodyguards—think she can handle that?"

AS *NELL* OPENED in movie theaters, not unexpectedly its star was on TV, promoting her new picture. Given her stake in the picture's success, though, her publicity campaign for it was a model of restraint; there were no Stupid Human Tricks on late-night television. She did, not surprisingly, do What Was Expected, making a single appearance on a prime-time magazine show ("Eye to Eye with Connie Chung") and on one of the morning chat programs ("Good Morning America") and setting aside a day or so to receive entertainment-press TV crews and print reporters from the larger papers in a carefully lighted and appointed room in one of the few Beverly Hills hotels (usually the Beverly Hilton, the Century Plaza, or the Four Seasons) that specializes in catering to movie-studio publicity machines and junketeering entertainment press. The crews and the reporters would be allotted a few minutes each; under those circumstances there was no time to ask anything other than the same few questions that everyone else was asking.

That's why, no matter who was asking the questions, the quotes and the sound bites were almost always the same. It's why, whether

you saw her on "E!," "E.T.," "Extra," or the entertainment segment of your local news, she would be wearing essentially the same
outfit (a loosely tied paisley-pattern scarf, the same one she wore
in most of the *Sommersby* interviews, over a silk shirt; the jeans
she had on usually weren't in the shot), sitting on the same sofa
or in the same chair in the same room—in the same medium camera shot, framing her with the same warmly glowing lampshade,
the same pink violets, the same green hanging plant, the same
rose-colored throw pillow. Usually, too, in interview after interview, she had the same few things to say.

She was, she would usually say with a small smile, a "kind of
urban, television-watching sort of modern girl, who's cynical and
doesn't put a lampshade on her head when she goes to a party.

"I mean, I'm not very emotionally accessible. . . . That was the
big revelation for me, that it wasn't that hard for me to be this
emotionally accessible. . . . It means"—another small smile—
"maybe you can be that way, maybe, in the real world and not
get clobbered for it."

Whether it's Jodie Foster and her well-known list of *thou shalt
nots*, or some other show business figure looking for publicity
while controlling the agenda, the members of the entertainment
press, who after all have to live in some sort of modus vivendi with
the studios and the stars, have learned that they, too, risk getting
clobbered unless they bring up certain subjects gingerly, if at all.
This is true of celebrity journalists, too.

For example, in the "Eye to Eye" segment (titled "Acting Up,"
probably a droll but deniable reference to Act Up, the gay activist
organization), Connie Chung asks, with all the celebrity interviewer's meaningful intensity, "*What is it* that's important about
maintaining privacy?"

Answers Foster: work is a "nine to seven job" anyway, so why
would she want to bring it home? She's let the "Eye to Eye" crew
tape her in her office and in her car, and she's even obliged them
by doing a piece of business at the Los Angeles studio from where
Connie is coanchoring the news (because "she dreamed of being

a broadcaster," Connie fairly burbles, "we thought she'd get a kick out of going behind the scenes with us"), but there's a limit. "I could never do one of those magazine things where they come to your house and they take pictures of it. . . . I would die of embarrassment."

A few days later, in New York on a "Good Morning America" faux fireplace Christmas set, with the somnolent Charles Gibson looking as if he's about to nod off, she explains why it's so hard to define Nell: "One of the great human impulses is to label things, put them in boxes, so that we feel better about how we categorize something else. . . ."

And, during the *Nell* junket, there's more than one variation on this theme: *Is there anything, Jodie Foster the person, not the actress, needs to be more free about?*

"Yeah." Shrug. "I mean, admitting vulnerability. Sure. I mean, I'm always the first to say"—in a tiny voice—"'No, no, I'm OK, I'm fine.'

"It's not for me to admit, you know, pain or whatever—you know, people hurting my feelings. I always have to act like I'm above it." Shrug. "That's part of being a public figure, too, where people say just virtually anything about you, and you do have to build some kind of armor, I guess."

In a mid-1992 survey of twenty-five hundred schoolgirls, from kindergarten through twelfth grade, who were asked to pick the Woman of the Year, Jodie Foster was the most named show business figure, ranking ahead of Madonna—and behind, in ascending order, Anita Hill, Mother Teresa, figure skater Kristi Yamaguchi, Barbara Bush, and, at the top of the list, "Mom."[25]

To her most immediate peers—Hollywood's twenty- and thirtysomething young actresses, many of whom are unfamiliar with Foster's career missteps and struggles in the eighties, she's a figure of something approaching awe. To Jennifer Jason Leigh (*Mrs. Parker and the Vicious Circle, Flesh & Blood, Miami Blues*), for example, she's a "brilliant actress and a smart woman." For

Rosanna Arquette (*The Executioner's Song, Black Rainbow, Desperately Seeking Susan*), Jodie is "one of my heroes. . . . She's so incredibly intelligent. . . . You look at most of the child stars and they either become drug addicts or commit suicide or some horrible tragedy [befalls them]. This is somebody that's well educated, that stops her career to do her education and is . . . just a serious person. I'd love to work with her as a director."

How high are Hollywood's expectations for Jodie Foster? By the early nineties she was already in the "club," as the late Paul Rosenfield characterized the Hollywood establishment in his insightful *The Club Rules* (Warner Books, 1992). "The club admires her," Rosenfield wrote, "because she didn't go under during the John Hinckley mess and become the answer to a trivia question. The club also likes her straightforward style."

Jodie Foster is now regularly included in roundups of pop culture's most influential people. In *Entertainment Weekly*'s 1994 ranking of the 101 most powerful figures in Hollywood, for example, she's number fifty-five, two steps below Julia Roberts, fourteen below Mel Gibson, eighteen below Clint Eastwood, twenty-four below Barbra Streisand, thirty-three below Tom Cruise, and thirty-nine below Tom Hanks.[26]

Nonetheless, she and Streisand, two decades her senior, are the only female actor-director-producer hyphenates on the entire list; there's not another woman, and very few of either gender, with that kind of multifaceted available control. Her "debit," according to the pop magazine's snide and safely anonymous handicappers: she hasn't cured cancer yet.

Then again, she hasn't stopped a deadly outbreak of an exotic fatal virus yet either—which is not to say that she can't. At least on screen. Jodie Foster has, however, chosen to make first contact with aliens instead.

Nine-year-old Jodie Foster, making the publicity rounds for her brand-new TV series "Paper Moon," told one interviewer she had a crush on Robert Redford, "just like every other girl."[27] Two decades later, in midsummer 1994, she dropped out of a film project, just days before it was scheduled to start shooting, that would have brought them together as costars. Her spokesperson cited script difficulties, while "sources" said that a script rewrite had diminished her role.[28]

(Foster has long been known as a stickler about scripts—as well she should be, given Hollywood's customarily cavalier attitude toward such matters as plot and characterization. *Nell*, for example, went through eight rewrites.)

The movie she rejected was *Crisis in the Hot Zone*, based on a 1992 *New Yorker* magazine article, a truth-is-scarier-than-fiction horror story chronicling an actual outbreak of the deadly and highly contagious ebola virus in the United States, just outside Washington, D.C., and a medical/military team's secret efforts to contain it.

Even before Foster turned cold on it, *Hot Zone* had become something of a Hollywood crisis itself. The high concept at the center of it—killer microbes—had spawned a competing project, *Outbreak*, fictionalizing the actual *Hot Zone* story. Competing teams of writers were racing to complete scripts, while competing producers—Lynda Obst, among others, for Twentieth Century Fox's *Hot Zone* and Arnold Kopelson for Warner Brothers' *Outbreak*—raced to line up stars, star directors, and other bankable elements.

Foster's pullout, however, was a deal breaker, and it was followed shortly by Redford's departure. Despite its "better" credentials (it was the original and it was based on a true story), the *Hot Zone* project, which was to have been directed by Ridley Scott, collapsed, clearing the way for the competing picture, starring Dustin Hoffman and directed by Wolfgang Peterson, to go into production for a 1995 release.

Months of frantic and concentrated effort and scores of thousands of dollars had been spent to no avail. But this was Hollywood, and if there was rancor or recrimination, it wasn't allowed to get in the way of doing business.

By autumn 1994, inside-industry word was that Lynda Obst would be producing Jodie Foster's next big picture, for Warner. *Contact*, based on Carl Sagan's bestselling science fiction novel, will be directed by George Miller (of the *Mad Max* trilogy) and, at this writing, will indeed star Foster as a radio astronomer convinced of the possibility of communicating with extraterrestrial life.

Talk of a Seberg biography has stopped, and in its place are the first stirrings of an even more fascinating film project: a biography of Leni Riefenstahl, a thirties film actress in Germany who became infamous as Hitler's favorite director and is best known for *Triumph of the Will*, a classic of both propaganda and documentary. On the set of *Nell*, Foster, watching a recent Riefenstahl film documentary on a VCR in her trailer, mused that the nonagenarian must regret making *Triumph* and not going to Holly-wood in the thirties when she had the chance.[29]

If the movie actually is made, it will be a risky role for Foster herself to take: Riefenstahl's insistence that aesthetics, not politics, motivated her can't help reigniting the debate about the connection between Foster's own personal and professional lives.

In another nice bit of symmetry that the industry is sure to appreciate, Foster currently rents Bette Davis's old Hollywood apartment when she's in L.A.

Her *Nell* performance did result in the expected Oscar nomination, and, perhaps not coincidentally, the 1995 award season coincided with new dish about Jodie Foster: this time the hot morsel was that she finally had a live-in lover . . .

A man.

True? False? Time, and the supermarket tabloids, will tell.

Early in the year she set up in Baltimore for location filming on *Home for the Holidays*, starring Holly Hunter, who survived her walk-on in *Svengali* to become the Best Actress of 1993 for *The Piano*.

(In the publicity buildup preceding that picture's release, one unnamed male studio executive, quoted on the paucity of good roles for women, said, "Holly Hunter is up for the same roles that Jodie Foster is considered for, and because Jodie Foster is a star, well, who would you rather have in your movie?"[30]).

Also in the *Holidays* cast are Anne Bancroft, Robert Downey, Jr., Charles Durning, Cynthia Stevenson, Steve Guttenberg, Dylan McDermott, and Claire Danes. The movie, Foster says, is about an "art restorer on the eve of the worst day of her life, and she has to go to the Thanksgiving from hell."[31]

Hunter plays a Chicago art restorer returning home to her Baltimore family. Bancroft is her mother; Durning her father; Downey and Stevenson, her brother and sister; Danes, her daughter; Guttenberg, her brother-in-law; and McDermott, a family friend and potential love interest.

The picture, written by W. D. Richter (*Brubaker*), was set originally in Boston, but, just as location scouting was about to get under way, the Maryland Film Commission threw a $16,000 reception on the yacht *Pride of Baltimore*, then fortuitously cruising Los Angeles harbor, that attracted Foster and, according to the picture's producer, Peggy Rajski, "certainly played a role" in the decision to relocate the Thanksgiving from hell to Baltimore.[32]

Early in the year the production set up temporary offices in an old firehouse that also housed the TV series "Homicide,"[33] whose executive producer, the film director Barry Levinson, is a Baltimore native. Soon the city's amazed residents, less sanguine than blasé Los Angelenos about celebrities in their midst, were spotting Foster in local coffee shops and even bumping into Sharon Stone, whose boyfriend is part of the *Holidays* crew, at a party at the National Aquarium.[34]

Jodie Foster, born a few days before the Thanksgiving holiday, has always presented herself as the down-to-earth craftsperson, the very opposite of a stagestruck actress. But in a deeper, more meaningful sense she *was* struck—in childhood, perhaps during those endless rehearsals with De Niro on *Taxi Driver*, by . . . something, something that has sparked into an enduring flame. One likes to picture her on that next set, making decisions and aesthetic choices, even finding time late at night, after dailies, in whatever Baltimore house she has rented for the duration, to read up on physics and radio astronomy. Ultraorganized and superbly well prepared. Happy.

Movie sets, she said late in 1994, are the "foundation of my life, the only place I feel really confident."[35] Of her company, Egg Pictures, she's said repeatedly that it is intended to be a "breeding ground for new filmmakers and for a new kind of film-making that's much more director-oriented."

At the age of thirty-two, the extraordinary first act of her public life is behind her. She now commands at least $6 million for acting in a big-studio picture.[36]

Jodie Foster has had the career of an actor twice her age and is uniquely well positioned now to do things that have never before been done, both on screen and inside the business she understands so well. So far, though, the most a well-wisher can say is that the Eastwood strategy seems to be working. In the hero's progress, it's now scene two of the second act . . .

Los Angeles, California
March 1995

AFTERWORD

Oscar/Spirit

ONCE AGAIN THE OSCARS

were a sure thing. At the end of March 1995 the smart money was on *Forrest Gump* and Zemeckis, just as it had been on *Schindler's List* and Spielberg the year before. Tom Hanks, too, was the favorite to repeat as Best Actor, after winning for *Philadelphia*, for his deadpan portrayal of America's favorite upwardly mobile simpleton.

Only in the Best Actress category was there any suspense at all. True, Jessica Lange was heavily favored to win for *Blue Sky*, the Tony Richardson–directed movie that had been sitting on a bankvault shelf since the year Orion Pictures went bankrupt, the same year *The Silence of the Lambs* swept all the major Academy Awards. But while *Forrest Gump* as Best Picture, Tom Hanks as Best Actor, and Robert Zemeckis as Best Director had become an irresistible litany at the various precursors, from the Globes to SAG, so that by Oscar night there probably wasn't an office pool in all of

America where they weren't heavily favored to win, Lange hadn't swept *all* the precursor awards.

A few days before Hollywood's big, internationally televised show, Jodie Foster, away in Baltimore on the *Home for the Holidays* shoot, won the Actor, as the prize at the first annual Screen Actors Guild award show was named. And because the award was from her peers, the competition between Foster and Lange added a soupçon of suspense to the otherwise tedious, nearly three-and-half-hour-long television show. As it was, a bemused and gracious Lange, who thanked both her children and Orion Pictures in her brief acceptance speech, and within a week was saying that she planned to move back to her native Minnesota, took the Best Actress statuette just as the oddsmakers from London to Las Vegas had forecast.

(But the predictability of the major winners didn't keep this from being the most-watched Oscar telecast since 1983, viewed in more than thirty-one million U.S. homes, a full ten million more than NBC's hot new medical drama, "ER," the second-most-watched TV show in America that week.

Oscar is not only the second-most-watched "event" program on the planet, its audience exceeded only by the quadrennial soccer play-offs, but only the Super Bowl can command more than the $685,000 the network reportedly gets for a thirty-second advertisement during the Academy Awards.)

In the audience Jodie Foster, who had taken a few days off from directing her second movie to fly into Hollywood for Oscar night, as well as to cochair the Independent Spirit Awards held in nearby Santa Monica two days before, smiled, if rather thinly. For the Best Actress nominees it was always a long night.

Over the years, she'd descried awards and Hollywood's penchant for self-congratulations many times, but now she was a player, and of players certain things are expected. So like the other A-list movie stars present (including her *Holidays* leading lady Holly Hunter, voted Best Actress just one year before), who were in effect the cutaway chorus for the TV cameras, she endured. And perhaps on this particular night she even maintained more than the appearance of politely amused interest. After all, a good friend—her date for the big night, in fact—was up for an Oscar, too.

Earlier that afternoon Jodie Foster, elegant in a beaded Armani sheath, and her tuxedoed escort, Randy Stone, a man of vaguely Don Johnson–ish good looks, had made their way down the red-carpeted press gauntlet, accompanied by her longtime publicist, a sharp-eyed blond woman in sunglasses, who knew just exactly at which of the many media stations flanking the celebrities' promenade her client should stop. When she did pause for brief, and usually bubbly, interviews, telling one questioner for example that she was "not interested particularly" in directing films in the future in which she would also act, her date often stood just behind her, his hand sometimes familiarly encircling her waist in a way that casually suggested intimacy.

Were they—? the press buzzed among themselves, *Was she*—? But no one asked, and she didn't tell.

Of course, that week they both were to be found in at least one magazine, albeit as the subjects of two separate articles. And despite the fact that the magazine was *The Advocate*, perhaps the most mainstream of the gay-oriented periodicals, there was no attempt at connecting the dots.

Foster (no doubt to her and her publicist's dismay) shared the magazine's cover with actor John Travolta. Inside, the story used the "rumors" about their sexualities (as well as those of Tom Cruise and Richard Gere) as a hook to call Hollywood the "last frontier in terms of being gay" and to ask rhetorically, "Who will test the movie industry" by coming out?[1] Noting Foster and Travolta's respective acting nominations, *The Advocate* story cited their careers as the "ultimate proof of the harmlessness of rumors."[2]

An item in "The Buzz" column in the same issue saluted *Trevor*, then a nominee for Best Achievement in Live Action Short Film, a "coming out story produced by Randy Stone and Peggy Rajski

. . . [that] captures the sometimes painful life of a gay teenager." What neither the item nor the cover story noted were Foster's connections with the two producers of the much-honored eighteen-minute gay-positive film.

Rajski was also producing Foster's *Home for the Holidays*. When *Trevor* tied for the live-action-short Oscar (with the drolly witty short film from Scotland, *Franz Kafka's It's a Wonderful Life*), Stone—not merely Foster's Oscar date but also an Emmy-winning casting director (*Bill, Adam,* and *Switched at Birth* are among his many TV credits), as well as *Tate's* executive producer—saluted Foster in his acceptance speech.

At the rostrum, beaming, Stone thanked "my best friend, Jodie," adding, "She supports both of us. Peggy's producing Jodie's next movie, I'm Jodie's date. She brought me good luck."

Later, after the annual exercise in televised interminability was finally over, Jodie and Randy made the party rounds, showing up briefly first at the $500-a-ticket Governors Ball at the Shrine Auditorium, where the show itself was held and chef Wolfgang Puck's menu featured Oscar-shaped roast salmon. Then it was on to the *Pulp Fiction* party, one of the last ever to be held at the venerable Chasen's restaurant, known most widely because of ex-president Ronald Reagan's well-publicized cravings for its house chili, which was about to close its doors after a half century in West Hollywood to make way for a mall.

The Chasen's party was a photographer's feast. Madonna posed with writer/director Quentin Tarantino, Courtney Love mugged with her doppelganger date, actress Amanda de Cadanet, whom she waspishly introduced as "my lesbian girlfriend." Among the thousand-plus celebrants were also John Travolta, Samuel L. Jackson, Sharon Stone (who caused a brief stir by insisting that her armed bodyguard also be allowed inside), Angela Bassett, Holly Hunter, Jay Leno, Julie Delpy, and Ellen Barkin.

A photographer there snapped a shot of Foster and Randy Stone, each with a hand clasping his Oscar: as ever, she's aware of the camera, smiling and looking directly up into its lens, while he leans over her, fondly kissing the top of her head.

Another year, another Armani outfit at another Oscar show. What was Jodie Foster thinking as she sat in the Shrine audience, politely applauding speech after predictable speech, listening to the overproduced song-and-dance numbers that seemed unchanged from the fifties, watching host Dave Letterman do a variation on his late-night TV shtick, complete with stupid pet trick? On certain rare occasions journalistic mind reading is easy:

Almost six weeks into production and location shooting on *Home for the Holidays*, the satisfying minutiae and details that a director always needs to sort out on a daily basis—how to make Baltimore's airport look like Chicago's O'Hare, for example—couldn't have been absent from her thoughts. She was too much the workaholic perfectionist for that. In fact, one result of a Directors Guild of America campaign to recruit union "hold-outs," who included both Quentin Tarantino and Spike Lee, was that she'd just applied for a membership in the guild herself,[3] and her Baltimore shoot was proceeding under DGA contract. Word of her guild application had surfaced around the same time that Foster struck a distribution deal for *Holidays* with Paramount Pictures, like all the big studios a guild signatory. Under the deal's terms Paramount would distribute her movie, scheduled for a November 1995 release, theatrically in North and South America, while Polygram Filmed Entertainment, which finances Foster's Egg Pictures, retained international distribution and domestic video and pay-TV rights. Paramount chairman Sherry Lansing, who'd produced *The Accused*, was said to be a "significant factor" in the *Holidays* decision, which marked Paramount's first distribution deal with Polygram.[4]

How could the sexuality issue, too, have failed to cross Foster's mind? A few days before the Oscars, the shotgun murder of a gay man by a straight male talk show guest, who'd been publicly "humiliated" on air when the gay man had revealed his "crush," had set off a debate not only about "ambush journalism" and careless talk show stunts but also about "lesbians and gay men [who] deplore outing with more fervor than they condemn the closet. . . . When lesbians and gay men wait for heterosexuals to create a safe society before affirming their identities, this is the result," as a passionate letter printed in the local newspaper on Oscar day put it.[5] Then there were *The Advocate* cover and *Trevor's* subject matter, and the whole glittery night must have been connected with the possibility of personal confrontation and threatened exposure anyway—at least since the Great Outing Campaign of '92.

Was Jodie Foster able to resist reflecting, during this long night of live-from-Los-Angeles mythmaking and cinematic idol worship, about the dangerous love of her more ardent fans? True, there was, as always, Hinckley.

Now she had to contend with the new possibility of a book penned by him or even a movie or TV miniseries that included his life story.

Just a month before, his attorneys had reached a negotiated settlement with former presidential press secretary James S. Brady and the two law-enforcement officers injured in the 1981 attempted assassination. Under its terms Hinckley would "surrender all legal rights to his life story to a trust controlled by [the three men he'd wounded],"[6] thereby potentially compensating them up to the agreed-on amount of $2.9 million, the most that the sale of his "rights" would conceivably bring. While no book or movie deal was announced then, the settlement opened the way for one; another provision of his settlement with the men he'd shot limited any personal benefit to Hinckley himself from any future deal to just $3,000 per year while he remained incarcerated and $12,000 per year if he was ever released from the mental hospital where he's spent the past decade and a half.

But there was another frightening public incident to ponder that glittery night, one that never made the papers despite the nearby presence of a large contingent from the press. On Oscar night it still must have been fresh as the ocean breeze of just two days before in Jodie Foster's mind.

In their tenth year the IFP/West Independent Spirit Awards, held in Los Angeles just two days before the Academy Awards for the purpose of honoring independent films and filmmakers, and attracting attention to them, were more mainstream than ever before.

On that bright and breezy Saturday afternoon before the Oscars, several hundred people gathered under a billowing white tent—a reminder, perhaps, of pre-air-conditioning Golden Era Hollywood and its penchant for elegant outdoor parties in big tents. This tent was pitched in a parking lot beside the glittering sea, and the guests could expect a casual catered lunch, speeches unconstrained by a timer and a flashing red light, and the Spirit Awards themselves. Not only were the eventual winners in all major categories present—most notably the cast, director, and producer of the biggest winner of the day, *Pulp Fiction*, and Linda Fiorentino, who won the Best Actress award for her sizzling portrayal in *The Last Seduction*—but such distinctly mainstream movie stars as Kim Basinger and Alec Baldwin also turned up.

Where once the independents all could fit cozily into a Sunset Boulevard restaurant for the awards, the invitations advised "dress jazzy," and most of the filmmakers there would be unfamiliar to any but the purest of cineasts, now big-name pictures and marquee-name actors vied for Spirit Awards, studios and talent agencies paid up to $10,000 for a table at the awards luncheon, and honest-to-goodness movie stars drove out to the beach on a brilliantly sunny Saturday afternoon just to attend. And while there still were no Oscar-style dancers and big production numbers, the TV networks were interested in televising this show too. In part the new cachet and visibility reflected the schizophrenic nature of "independent" filmmaking in the midnineties.

Independent success already had attracted big-studio attention

. . . and big-studio dollars. By 1995 the best and the brightest of the "independent" companies (Miramax, Fine Line, Jersey) all were owned outright or financed by major Hollywood players—Disney, Turner, and Tri-Star, respectively, and who or what was truly an independent was no longer so simple to define. Appropriately, Foster, the ultimate insider's outsider, had long been associated with this filmmakers' group, now much preoccupied with its own identity crisis. But as ever, she knew where she was going. As film critic Roger Ebert puts it, "I think she does have a strategy. I think she is singlemindedly determined not to become a female lead in male pictures, which is the career route that so many actresses are trapped by. . . .

"I've always felt that she will, sooner or later, wind up running a studio. She'll never leave the business, but I think she will only act on terms that are consistent with the career she's had."

In 1995 Jodie Foster, honorary cochair, was returning to the event that she'd also cochaired in 1992 and where, in 1989, her performance in *Five Corners* had won a Best Actress award. As before, her remarks at the Spirit Awards were brief, pointed, and could be taken as two-edged.

A big part of the annual Spirit ceremony, observed the woman who among all her peers was by far the most likely someday to run a major movie studio herself, is to "slag unmercifully those nasty studios." And while other speakers and award winners struggled with the oxymoronic definition of "Hollywood independence," Foster, having done her duty and made an appearance, slipped away.

While, increasingly, the nominees at the Spirit Awards also may be vying for the Hollywood establishment's own coveted statuette, fan access, security, and level of formality still remain defining differences between the two events.

The Academy Awards show is all about limousines, red carpets, and designer gowns; access is tightly controlled, and security reaches presidential levels. At the Spirit Awards, by contrast,

Keanu Reeves once showed up on his motorcycle, and most of the other celebrities still come in their own cars. At the 1995 edition of the Spirit Awards, there was security—around the parking lot tent, a platoon of burly young people dressed identically in black slacks and tight white T-shirts patrolled a loose perimeter, marked by the same type of knotted rope one sees in movie theater lobbies. But beyond this mostly symbolic perimeter a typically glorious day on the Santa Monica beach was unfolding in all its Mediterranean, carnival-on-the-bay, Felliniesque splendor.

Sunbathers lolled on the sand within sight of the arriving and departing stars, Spandexed rollerbladers flashed by, groups of sunscreen-slathered tourists laden with cameras and coolers trudged toward the shimmering beach. From just outside the tent the sussurant hiss of foaming waves mingled with the muffled shouts of little knots of the curious as they spotted a famous face. How close were the surprised and delighted fans, and how approachable the celebrities?

As actress Amanda Plummer, outside for a smoke, stepped to the roped-off perimeter around the big tent, two twentysomething young men wearing de rigueur baggy pants, oversize T-shirts, and backward baseball caps rushed up to her, one pleading for an autograph on the rolled-up *Pulp Fiction* poster he was carrying. "*Please. Sign it 'Honey Bunny,'*" he implored, handing her the poster and a pen. As she signed, abruptly he threw his arm around her shoulder and drew her closer to him, grinning broadly, while his companion pulled from his pocket a hidden small camera and snapped away. Spotting them, two security men quickly approached, but the two fans sprinted away, calling out "Thanks, Honey Bunny" as they dashed from sight and were soon lost among the parked cars.

Handing out the Spirit Awards themselves was just getting under way when Jodie Foster strode out alone, leaving the tent and the roped-off perimeter behind, a small, determined figure crossing the big parking lot to her car.

Later a policeman blamed the paparazzi, but the professional photographers said it wasn't they who caused it; it was the twitchy security people . . . and the fans.

"When she came out the side [of the big tent], there was no security there at all," says veteran celebrity photographer Gary Boas, who was right there on the scene with a few colleagues. "She was mobbed."

First a few disbelieving fans dashed across the beach toward her, then more . . . and more . . . and more. Soon her tiny figure was lost at the center of a clotted crowd of several dozen people, growing larger by the second. People were shouting out her name, taking her picture, shoving pen and paper at her. Quickly the professional photographers pushed their way to the front of this gathering chaos, their lenses just inches from her face. As she tried to move forward, the crowd moved slowly with her, the photographers backpedaling while continuing to shoot.

From the side of the tent a tall blond woman—her publicist—crossed the distance to her beleaguered client at a dead run. She pushed her way to her client's side and wrapped a protective arm around her shoulders. Together, still at the center of the tightly packed crowd, they reversed field, retreating back toward the tent, then cutting from one side of the parking lot to the other, trying to maneuver between the rows of parked cars. At the periphery excited people tripped and fell, but the crowd matched the star and the publicist motion for motion and turn for turn, like a flock of shore birds dashing en masse after a retreating wave. A couple of white-T-shirted security men, seeing the commotion, shoved their way through to her.

At last they made it to a car, a dark green Bronco, in the middle of the lot and jumped inside, Jodie behind the wheel. The fans and photographers, still shooting through the car's tinted windows, surrounded the parked automobile. After several long moments, with the crowd tightly packed all around the car, immobilizing it, half a dozen more security men appeared.

"She was mobbed by fans," continues Boas, who like all good veteran photographers in situations like this always heads for where he sees the fans rushing. He'd been sitting on the ground with his gear at the tent's main entrance, waiting for the celebrities to leave. "The fans were the first [to spot her]. As soon as I saw them dart, I got up. I knew from past years that [Jodie] usually leaves right after she does her thing. There she was. . . .

"She was signing [autographs]," the photographer continues, "but everybody else was making a big deal. All of a sudden [her publicist] came out, and she started pushing her away and then security darted around the corner, and *they* started pushing her away. . . .

"I'm sure for her it was scary."

The security reinforcements pushed the crowd, some of the fans still excitedly calling out her name, back from the car, and the publicist hopped out. Jodie, a tiny figure barely visible behind the wheel of the big car, gunned it, racing out of the parking lot and down the access road leading back to the Santa Monica street. Soon she was gone. Inside the big tent, the award-show party went on.

Watching the car disappearing out into the busy beachfront traffic, one of the security men shook his head in disbelief. "They brought her out unattended, and they mobbed her," he said heatedly. "*We* woulda escorted her to the car, but they didn't tell *us* anything. She just came out. It was pretty scary. I'll bet she never does *that* again."

Perhaps. But then again, this was Jodie Foster, who, next to excellence, always has craved some semblance of normality, always has been a woman determined to direct her own life.

NOTES

Introduction: Interview and Overview

1. *Long Beach Press-Telegram,* May 30, 1989.
2. Mason Wiley and Damien Bona, *Inside Oscar: The Unofficial History of the Academy Awards* (New York: Ballantine Books, 1993), 747.

Kid Stuff

1. *American Film,* October 1988.
2. *People,* May 19, 1980.
3. *Seventeen,* January 1977.
4. *After Dark,* July 1980.
5. *American Film,* October 1988.
6. *Interview,* October 1991.
7. Ibid.
8. *TV Guide,* November 16, 1974.
9. *Vanity Fair,* September 1988.
10. *American Premiere,* October–November 1988.
11. *Cosmopolitan,* August 1977.

12. *Interview*, January 1977.

13. Les Keyser, *Martin Scorsese* (New York: Twayne Publishers, 1992), 78. The internal quote is from Kevin Jackson, ed., *Schrader on Schrader* (New York: Faber & Faber, 1990), 120.

14. *Village View*, February 15–21, 1991.

15. Joel Eisner and David Krinsky, *Television Comedy Series: An Episode Guide to 153 TV Sitcoms in Syndication* (Jefferson, North Carolina: McFarland & Company, 1984), 655.

16. Vincent Terrace, *Encyclopedia of Television Series, Pilots and Specials, Volume I: 1937–1973* (New York: New York Zoetrope, 1986), 313.

17. Damien Bona, *Opening Shots* (New York: Workman Publishing, 1994), 147.

18. *American Film*, October 1988.

19. *Cosmopolitan*, February 1989.

20. *Interview*, January 1977.

21. *San Francisco Sunday Examiner & Chronicle*, March 11, 1984.

22. *Los Angeles Herald-Examiner*, September 26, 1974.

23. *TV Guide*, September 21, 1974.

24. *The Hollywood Reporter*, November 12, 1974.

25. *After Dark*, July 1980.

26. *TV Guide*, November 16, 1974.

27. Mick Martin and Marsha Porter, ed., *Video Movie Guide* (New York: Ballantine Books, 1994), 611.

28. *Daily Variety*, December 15, 1980.

29. *Daily Variety*, July 7, 1972.

30. *Interview*, January 1977.

31. Ibid.

32. *Interview*, September 1989.

33. *Daily Variety*, July 7, 1972.

34. *Daily Variety* and *The Hollywood Reporter*, both March 6, 1973.

35. *The Hollywood Reporter*, June 8, 1973.

36. *Vanity Fair*, May 1994.

37. *Time*, February 23, 1976.

The Taxi Driver and the Little Girl

1. *US*, March 4, 1980.
2. *Los Angeles Times*, June 4, 1981.
3. Ibid.
4. *Interview*, August 1987.
5. *American Premiere*, October–November 1988.
6. *Time*, February 23, 1976.
7. *The Canyon Crier*, February 7, 1977.
8. Mason Wiley and Damien Bona, *Inside Oscar: The Unofficial History of the Academy Awards* (New York: Ballantine Books, 1993), 525.
9. *Los Angeles Herald-Examiner*, April 7, 1981.
10. *Los Angeles Times*, March 1, 1976.
11. *Cosmopolitan*, August 1977.
12. *New York Times*, March 7, 1976.
13. *Los Angeles Times*, March 1, 1976.
14. *Seventeen*, January 1977.
15. *Family Weekly*, April 16, 1978.
16. Charles Champlin in the *Los Angeles Times*, May 28, 1976.
17. *The Hollywood Reporter*, September 13, 1977.
18. *Interview*, January 1977.
19. "*The South Bank Show*," 1990.
20. *Time*, August 30, 1976.
21. *American Premiere*, October–November 1988.
22. *Cosmopolitan*, August 1977.
23. Ibid.

Euroteen/Valley Girl

1. *Variety*, November 16, 1977.
2. *Variety*, June 24, 1977.
3. *Family Weekly*, April 16, 1978.
4. Marilyn Beck in the *Los Angeles Herald-Examiner*, February 16, 1977.

5. *US*, March 4, 1980.
6. *People*, May 19, 1980.
7. *Newsweek*, August 1, 1977.
8. *Variety*, October 22, 1980.
9. *Variety*, November 16, 1977.
10. *People*, December 12, 1977.
11. *Inside Hollywood*, July–August 1991.
12. *Seventeen*, February 1978.
13. *People*, June 30, 1980.
14. *People*, May 19, 1980.
15. *US*, March 4, 1980.
16. *People*, June 30, 1980.
17. Andy Warhol in *Interview*, June 1980.
18. Patrick Pacheco in *After Dark*, July 1980.
19. Ibid.
20. Richard Stayton in the *Los Angeles Times*, April 1, 1994.

Flashback

1. *After Dark*, July 1980.
2. *Esquire*, October 1980.
3. *Interview*, May 1981.
4. *Los Angeles Times Magazine*, December 11, 1994.
5. *New York Times*, March 16, 1981.
6. *Newsweek*, April 6, 1981.
7. *Los Angeles Herald-Examiner*, April 1, 1981.
8. *Los Angeles Herald-Examiner*, April 2, 1981.
9. Lincoln Caplan in *The New Yorker*, July 7, 1984, 46, 48. This article was later expanded to book length. Titled *The Insanity Defense and the Trial of John W. Hinckley, Jr.*, it was published by David R. Godine, Boston, 1984.
10. *Los Angeles Times*, April 2, 1981.

11. *Los Angeles Herald-Examiner,* April 2, 1981.

12. Ibid.

13. *Los Angeles Times,* April 2, 1981.

14. *Los Angeles Herald-Examiner,* April 4, 1981.

15. *New York Times,* September 30, 1981.

16. Ibid.

17. Caplan, *The New Yorker,* 50.

18. Garry Wills, *Reagan's America: Innocents at Home* (Garden City, NY: Doubleday & Company, 1987), 210.

19. Herbert L. Abrams, *The President Has Been Shot: Confusion, Disability and the 25th Amendment in the Aftermath of the Attempted Assassination of Ronald Reagan* (New York: W. W. Norton & Company, 1992), 22–23.

20. Ibid., 23.

21. Ibid., 24.

22. Ibid., 24.

23. Ibid., 24.

24. Caplan, *The New Yorker,* 56.

25. *New York Times,* April 5, 1981.

26. Caplan, *The New Yorker,* 60.

27. Caplan, *The New Yorker,* 57.

28. *New York Times,* April 8, 1981.

29. *New York Times,* April 9, 1981.

30. Jodie Foster in *Esquire,* December 1982.

31. Ibid.

32. *New York Times,* April 9, 1981.

33. *Los Angeles Herald-Examiner,* January 8, 1984.

34. *Los Angeles Times,* December 9, 1983.

35. *People,* April 20, 1981.

36. Peter J. Boyer in the *Los Angeles Times,* June 4, 1981.

37. Ibid.

38. *People,* April 20, 1981.

39. Boyer, *Los Angeles Times.*

A Continuing Education

1. *TV Guide*, November 16, 1974.
2. Jodie Foster in *Esquire*, December 1982.
3. Ibid.
4. *US*, October 10, 1983.
5. *Film Comment*, September–October 1982.
6. *Los Angeles Times*, August 26, 1982.
7. Foster, *Esquire*.
8. *Los Angeles Times*, March 9, 1983.
9. *Newsweek*, February 8, 1982.
10. *Los Angeles Times*, May 13, 1982.
11. *United Press International*, February 19, 1983.
12. Foster, *Esquire*.
13. *San Francisco Sunday Examiner and Chronicle*, March 11, 1984.
14. *Los Angeles Times*, September 11, 1983.
15. *Interview*, August 1987.
16. *Vanity Fair*, May 1984.
17. *Village View*, February 15-21, 1991.
18. *TV Guide*, August 11, 1984.
19. *Los Angeles Times*, September 11, 1983.
20. Edward Guthmann in the *San Francisco Sunday Examiner and Chronicle*, March 11, 1984.
21. *Mademoiselle*, May 1984.
22. *Variety*, July 18, 1984.
23. Ibid.
24. *Premiere*, March 1991.
25. *Los Angeles Times*, October 6, 1991.
26. *New York Times*, January 6, 1991.
27. *Interview*, August 1987.
28. Ibid.
29. Ibid.
30. *Mademoiselle*, September 1987.
31. *Movieline*, November 6, 1987.

32. John H. Richardson in the *Los Angeles Daily News,* November 26, 1987.
33. J. Hoberman in the *Village Voice,* November 24, 1987.
34. *Entertainment Weekly,* April 2, 1993.
35. *Mademoiselle,* September 1987.
36. *Elle,* March 1987.
37. *Vanity Fair,* September 1988.
38. Ibid.
39. Susan Royal in *American Premiere,* October–November 1988.
40. *Mademoiselle,* September 1987.
41. *Glamour,* October 1987.

Oscar and Innuendo

1. *Vanity Fair,* September 1988.
2. *Entertainment Weekly,* April 2, 1993.
3. *American Film,* October 1988.
4. Ibid.
5. *Rolling Stone,* March 21, 1991.
6. *American Film,* October 1988.
7. *Premiere,* March 1991.
8. *American Film,* October 1988.
9. *The Cable Guide,* November 1989.
10. *Premiere,* March 1991.
11. *American Film,* October 1988.
12. Dan Yakir in *Interview,* August 1987.
13. Ibid.
14. Ibid.
15. *Entertainment Weekly,* April 2, 1993.
16. Ibid.
17. *Daily Variety,* May 10, 1989.
18. Mason Wiley and Damien Bona, *Inside Oscar: The Unofficial History of the Academy Awards* (New York: Ballantine Books, 1993), 736.

19. Ibid., 746.

20. Ibid., 747.

21. Ibid., 747.

22. *The Cable Guide*, November 1989.

23. Ibid.

24. Michael A. Lerner in *Interview*, September 1989.

25. Yakir, *Interview*.

26. *Inside Hollywood*, July–August 1991.

27. *Vogue*, February 1991.

Whiz Kid Redux

1. *Elle*, March 1987.

2. Ibid.

3. *Interview*, September 1989.

4. *Premiere*, March 1991.

5. J. D. Salinger, *Franny and Zooey* (Boston; Little, Brown and Company, 1961), 54.

6. Duane Byrge in *The Hollywood Reporter*, September 3, 1991.

7. *Redbook*, November 1991.

8. *Harper's Bazaar*, November 1991.

9. *Rolling Stone*, March 21, 1991.

10. *Los Angeles Times*, October 6, 1991.

11. Ibid.

12. *Interview*, October 1991.

13. Joe Levy in the *Los Angeles Daily News*, August 21, 1990.

14. *Village Voice*, February 15–21, 1991.

15. Ibid.

16. *Premiere*, March 1991.

17. *Interview*, October 1991.

18. Ibid.

19. *Tower Video Collector*, June–July 1991.

20. Jonathan Van Meter in the *New York Times Magazine*, January 6, 1991.

21. *Daily Variety*, August 28, 1990.
22. Ibid.
23. *Daily Variety*, December 12, 1990.
24. *The Hollywood Reporter*, September 18, 1991.

The Silence and the Shouting

1. *Village View*, February 15-21, 1991.
2. *London Sunday Times*, May 12, 1991.
3. *Premiere*, March 1991.
4. *Los Angeles Times*, December 4, 1992.
5. *Daily Variety*, September 16, 1981.
6. *Rolling Stone*, March 21, 1991.
7. Bob Strauss in the *Tower Video Collector*, June–July 1991.
8. *Inside Hollywood*, July–August 1991.
9. Strauss, *Tower Video Collector*.
10. Ibid.
11. *Premiere*, March 1991.
12. Ibid.
13. *Vanity Fair*, May 1994.
14. *Los Angeles Times*, May 29, 1992.
15. *Village Voice*, March 12, 1991.
16. Ibid.
17. *Village Voice*, April 16, 1991.
18. *Los Angeles Times*, April 1, 1992.

Hollywood's Maverick

1. *Variety*, February 2, 1995.
2. *Daily Variety*, October 21, 1992.
3. *In Style*, September 1993.
4. Kenneth Turan in the *Los Angeles Times*, February 5, 1993.
5. *The Hollywood Reporter*, February 8, 1993.

6. William Kissel in the *Los Angeles Times*, March 30, 1993.
7. *Sunday London Times*, May 12, 1991.
8. *Daily Variety*, February 14, 1992.
9. *Screen International*, May 21, 1993.
10. *Daily Variety*, March 15, 1993.
11. *The Hollywood Reporter*, April 20, 1992.
12. *Vanity Fair*, May 1994.
13. Ibid.
14. *Premiere*, June 1994.
15. Ibid.
16. *Vanity Fair*, May 1994.
17. *Square Peg*, March–April 1993.
18. *Los Angeles Times Magazine*, December 11, 1994.
19. Ibid.
20. *Entertainment Weekly*, April 2, 1993.
21. *The Hollywood Reporter*, December 23, 1994.
22. *Los Angeles Reader*, December 16, 1994.
23. *New York Times*, December 14, 1994.
24. *The Hollywood Reporter*, January 6-8, 1995.
25. *Los Angeles Times*, June 15, 1992.
26. *Entertainment Weekly*, October 28, 1994.
27. *Los Angeles Herald-Examiner*, September 26, 1974.
28. *Daily Variety*, July 14, 1994.
29. *Premiere*, January 1995.
30. *Los Angeles Times*, November 14, 1993.
31. *Philadelphia Inquirer*, December 25, 1994.
32. *Baltimore Sun*, February 13, 1995.
33. *Baltimore Sun*, January 24, 1995.
34. *Baltimore Sun*, February 24, 1995.
35. *New York Times*, December 12, 1994.
36. *Harper's Bazaar*, January 1995.

Afterword: Oscar Spirit

1. *The Advocate*, April 4, 1995.
2. Ibid.
3. *The Hollywood Reporter*, March 6, 1995.
4. *Variety*, March 8, 1995.
5. *Los Angeles Times*, March 27, 1995.
6. *Los Angeles Times*, February 24, 1995.

FILMOGRAPHY

MOST LISTS* OF JODIE Foster's films generally begin with *Napoleon and Samantha*.

While they often include her later TV projects, such as *Svengali*, the early movies for television, including the three "ABC Afternoon Specials" and *Smile, Jenny, You're Dead*, are omitted, as are *The Fisherman and His Wife*, an animated movie for which she did voice-over narration, and *It Was a Wonderful Life*, a documentary about homeless women that she also narrated.

Following that convention, these are the films of Jodie Foster:

1972   *Napoleon and Samantha*
1972   *Kansas City Bomber*
1973   *Tom Sawyer*
1973   *One Little Indian*

*In a few instances film dates may vary from list to list by up to a year.

1975	*Alice Doesn't Live Here Anymore*
1976	*Echoes of a Summer*
1976	*Taxi Driver*
1976	*Bugsy Malone*
1976	*The Little Girl Who Lives Down the Lane*
1977	*Il Casotto*
1977	*Moi, Fleur Bleue*
1977	*Freaky Friday*
1978	*Candleshoe*
1980	*Carny*
1980	*Foxes*
1983	*O'Hara's Wife*
1983	*Svengali*
1984	*The Hotel New Hampshire*
1984	*Le Sang des Autres*
1986	*Mesmerized* (also coproduced)
1987	*Siesta*
1988	*Five Corners*
1988	*Stealing Home*
1988	*The Accused*
1990	*Backtrack*
1991	*The Silence of the Lambs*
1991	*Little Man Tate* (also directed)
1992	*Shadows and Fog*
1993	*Sommersby*
1994	*Maverick*
1994	*Nell* (also produced)
1995	*Home for the Holidays* (directing and producing only; tentative title and release date)
1996	*Contact* (projected release date)

INDEX